WHERE DO COMEDIANS GO WHEN THEY DIE?

MILTON JONES

WHERE DO COMEDIANS GO WHEN THEY DIE?

JOURNEYS OF A STAND-UP

JR
BOOKS

First published in Great Britain in 2009 by
JR Books, 10 Greenland Street, London NW1 0ND
www.jrbooks.com

A catalogue record for this book is available from the British Library.

ISBN 978-1-906779-57-3

1 3 5 7 9 10 8 6 4 2

Printed by MPG Books, Bodmin, Cornwall

Acknowledgements

Well, I hope this works. Regardless of the outcome, thanks to my amazing wife Carol, and to my children, Adam, Jay and Amelia, for just being themselves and selling me their gags. Also, thanks to my parents for everything – look, you created a monster! And thanks to my brother Andy for . . . no, sorry, still can't think of anything. I'm also grateful to everyone involved in the publishing process – Jeremy Robson, Lesley Wilson and Chris Stone – and to my agent, Nick Ranceford-Hadley at Noel Gay, for getting things rolling. Not forgetting my fellow comedians – thanks for your company and inspiration. Come, let us stand together to fight hack comedy and plagiarism! We will fight them on the beaches . . . okay, forget the plagiarism thing. But thanks everyone. No, really.

Milton Jones

Preface

There is nothing in the world like the feeling of making lots of people laugh out loud all at once. There's also nothing in the world like the feeling of not making lots of people laugh at all, especially when they've been told that you're going to, and that this is what you do for a living.

It's a lonely racket, but it's also a way of life that has huge benefits. Apart from the laughter, the best bits of the job are the people you meet and the places you get to go. But these are also the worst bits of the job as well.

The performing itself is an intense experience and you'll only pull it off if you stay one step ahead of the crowd. This means that often you only realise what actually happened at a show on the way home or much later – that new laugh you got, the heckle you didn't quite deal with, or what to say next time to a party of 12 men who are all dressed as Elvis and are talking too much. (By the way it's 'Oi lads, a little less conversation'.) To represent this fractured state of mind the following journeys are described as they happen, but are also spliced together with flashbacks of what's just gone before, a bit like extra portions of rice that keep on arriving in an Indian restaurant, well after you've moved onto dessert.

Travelling, of course, can be instantly forgettable and you often arrive at a junction, station or airport with no recollection of ever having been there before, even though you must have been, many times. But as you travel between A and B on the great train of life, you do get the chance to reflect if you're actually going anywhere, or just arriving very slowly at Aberystwyth station. You see, comedians are always waiting for something, either to arrive or to take off.

This story isn't about the jokes, it's about the bits in between. Like all comics, the hero is appreciated by most of the people most of the time, and occasionally either irrationally adored or hated – neither for any good reason, usually. It may all be a bit less 'rock and roll' than you're expecting, but in another way it will probably be a lot scarier than you can imagine (unless you've played Dartmouth Naval Training College on a Friday night).

Perhaps I should be more interested in the science of my craft, how laughter works, and the complex psychology and physiology of what makes humans express elation in the form of abstract roars and sniffles. But like my audiences I don't care too much for formulas or 'recipes'. Besides, something that's cooked up once won't necessarily work again. It is essentially of the moment, to be consumed there and then – the right thing at the right time in the right place, you had to be there.

I just wanted to describe what it's like to try and make people laugh for a living, night after night in tiny clubs, huge theatres, on radio, television, in far away places and even when large men stop you in the street and demand that you tell them a joke. Because whatever happens you're on your own – it's either the dejected loneliness of failure, or the exhilarating isolation of success.

To succeed in this business you always have to be looking for a joke; always turning things upside down, holding them up to the light, and then smashing them on the ground to see if anything funny happens. This can be quite annoying to live with, apparently.

You see, I've also tried to write about how all this can affect your relationships with family, friends and with the increasing number of voices in your head. How, once you learn to paralyse that part of your brain that connects blind terror with its effects on your body, it can become a compulsion. A giant 'dare' that gets out of hand and drives you forward at an insatiable gallop until you either win a race or more likely come unstuck at one of the fences. All around are rider-less horses and unseated jockeys, but you can only hear the frightening commentary in your ear of how someone else is way out ahead. (Yes, you also become obsessed with sculpting huge and elaborate metaphors, and then relentlessly hammer them home long after they have ceased to have any meaning.) Of course the harder you try to succeed the harder it is to admit defeat, and even in fits of pique when you declare that this time you're really going to give up, the words seem to tumble out with all the unconvincing venom of a hotel hairdryer.

For most of us it's more than just a job where you can get free food, free beer and if you're not picky, free sex. It's a relationship in itself, a passionate on-off romance with ideas, people and the image you project of yourself. It's a game where you can make both instant friends and enemies. They know you, but you don't know them. And yet they don't really know you, but now you're not sure if you know yourself, either.

This is not the Diary of Anne Frank. Make no mistake, there have been far better people who have done nobler things in more difficult times. But this is the story of someone who did an odd job at a unique moment in history. Established orders were crumbling, cultures were clashing and the clowns stood tall in the mess. They were the dung beetles who rolled great big balls of the stuff and juggled them for money in far-flung places.

Although adjusting the facts a little is often an occupational necessity, much of what's described has not much more than a fake moustache and glasses to disguise its autobiographical nature. These are the thoughts of someone like me, in a world very similar to the one I know. The action happens over about 10 years, and all the events happened either to me, someone I know or someone I've completely made up. Some characters are two people welded together like a dodgy car. I hope, at least, they are roadworthy and that the absence of any traceable histories gets me off the hook with the people concerned.

But on the whole this is not some sort of autobiography, I'll save that for another life. People often ask me what it's like to do this job. Well, it's a bit like this . . .

WHERE DO
COMEDIANS GO
WHEN THEY DIE ?

City

May 2004: London, by foot and car

Noise, people, traffic – it's like Piccadilly Circus round here! It *is* Piccadilly Circus round here. Buses, taxis, tourists – it's like the 'London' of an American film, apart from the beggars, the fumes and a bubbling sense of menace. An unofficial conga shuffles along the pavement, funnelled by the railings and tinted with flickering neon, all to the beat of an unseen drum. Everyone is out, and looking for a Saturday night to remember.

Jed the bouncer grips my hand briefly as I pass through the entrance of the Comedy Lounge. The huge cellar is filling up with groups of friends, stag-parties, rugby fans (there was a match today), couples, loners, groups of loners, tinkers, tailors, soldiers, sailors, rich men but no poor men – not at £15 a time. They are about to become 'the audience' – a special one-off assembly, dependent on a thousand arbitrary decisions. Down the stairs I go, sidestepping through the queue, through the double-doors, across the front of the bar then through the door at the side of the stage and into the dressing room. This is where the battle-hardened contract killers assemble and load their weapons.

'How's it going Danny?' I say. 'Did Tina have that baby yet?'

'Little girl, two days ago!'

'Congratulations mate!'

'I've got photos!'

'Uh oh, here we go . . .'

These are my friends and we are all comedians.

But there's an unfamiliar face in the corner. I shake his hand, we all know the fear of being new, but he doesn't seem to have any (usually a bad sign). He's young and American, from 'Chicago, Illinois' (as opposed to all the other Chicagos).

He gives the MC, Danny Bullen, a list of credits to announce before he goes on stage. Danny and I exchange glances – British crowds are unimpressed by this sort of thing, it sounds like boasting. The Yank looks in the mirror and begins to gee himself up.

'Looking good buddy!'

Then he checks his clothes

'Turtle-neck, shoes, pants!'

Looking the other way, I can't help imagining a huge turtle coming ashore wearing only shoes and Y-fronts.

While Danny warms up the crowd out front, Eric Bowman and I are filling each other in on the other gigs we're doing this evening. Eric does this while crouching slightly, in his sharp navy suit, thrusting his chin towards the mirror and clipping out flecks of grey from his goatee with the tiny manicure scissors he keeps for this purpose. Everything about his appearance says that he's made an effort. He has a good Roman nose and dark brown eyes, but like most comics his features don't quite add up to good-looking. Rather he's learnt to use the sum of the parts to play both ugly and handsome, which is sometimes labelled as charisma.

I'm up first, and am watching Danny finish a routine on the TV monitor – a porthole to a different world. It's time to leave the decompression chamber and take my chances on the waves.

'Here we go, this is me . . .' I break off.

'Have a good one' says Eric unconvincingly.

In a moment of nervous solitude behind the black curtain I listen to Danny at work. I can't see him but I can feel him pacing back and forth, expertly feeding the microphone cable through his fingers, like an Alsatian pretending to be tethered. His words and the crowd's reaction make up a huge abstract symphony – the rhythm of the language, teasing and leading, a breath then a pause, but best of all, the gaps are compliantly filled with huge condensed roars of appreciation. There he stands, impudent, in his jeans and T-shirt, everything about his appearance says that he hasn't made an effort, that it's all entirely spontaneous. I smile, not because I haven't heard Danny's jokes a hundred times before, but because I don't think you ever get tired of the sound of joy. Now I want to play too.

'Our first act is a very good friend' he booms from the stage. 'One of the best acts on the comedy circuit today . . .'

This is me.

'Ladies and Gentlemen, Jerome Stevens!'

Smiling, I whip back the curtain, bound on to the stage and unravelling the cable I put the microphone to my lips.

'It's great to be here' I say, meaning it for possibly the first time in my career. You see, recently something happened to me on the other side of the world which made my life flash before my eyes.

One by one, I begin to introduce my lines like old friends to the crowd, awakening the beast. Will it be a contented pussycat or perhaps an injured leopard? I throw it a drunk Australian heckler early on – 'you see, this is why we sent them to Australia in the first place!' – laughter and applause. The creature gobbles him up and then purrs contentedly, for now.

For over a decade I've been doing this, bits of radio, telly – but mainly gigs, lots of gigs. New York, London, Paris, Melton Mowbray. I try not to talk to people from the audience, after a show. (Spaz Benson loves it, and he often stands by the door saying goodbye as they leave.) But everyone has an opinion about whether you're funny or not, and they'll often feel the need to tell you if they think you succeeded. For to try and make someone laugh is to attempt to win their affection, and if you fail – like a rejected suitor – they often think they owe you an explanation: 'You're not my type' or 'I'm seeing someone funnier'.

A man laughs in the wrong place. Now the rest laugh at him.
  'Try and keep up, will you' I say.
  The crowd laughs again. Then he laughs on his own again.
  'Okay fair enough, go at your own pace.'

Some can be gushing in their praise, but others tell you by what they omit. 'You had a good . . . slot on the bill didn't you?'
  Then there's the timid fan that just wants to talk. 'How did you get started? Where do you get your material?'
  The bargirl that couldn't see me earlier when I tried to get served, may now be smiling and trying to catch my eye. But it's best not to get involved, not to be rude or stylishly aloof because if you take their drinks and answer their questions their eyes soon glaze over, especially if you tell them the plain truth. The magic is broken.

The tiny red light facing me on the ceiling has come on. Twenty minutes has nearly gone already. Time to wrap it up.

For some there is even the shocking realisation that you're not making it up as you go along. 'You said a lot of those things last time I saw you.' (Yes, that's why it's called an 'act'.) Then there's the enthusiastic drunk who offers you another joke you can 'use', but you know before they start that you won't want to, and sure enough it always seems to go something like 'There were these three Pakis . . .'

'That's all from me – thank you and goodnight!'

Off the stage, through the dressing room, a nod to Liam the techy, then up the stairs two at a time – I've got to get round the whole city tonight. Now I'm running through Leicester Square, Oxford Street – the whole giant Monopoly set. Rickshaws, rotating crispy ducks, aromatic petrol fumes. If you think London has a big Chinatown you should see Shanghai! (Crispy ducks are easier to catch by the way, you can hear them coming.)

My car's up in Tottenham Court Road half a mile away but I'm due on stage in Palmers Green in four minutes and it's a half hour journey. Rod the compere said he would keep talking until I get there. These places look so close together on a map when you book them in your diary three months before.

Now I'm slaloming through a line of Hare Krishna devotees all banging their pots and pans, the leader has a cordless microphone headset – wonder if he claims that against tax? By Shaftesbury Avenue my feet are warming up inside my trainers, but my lungs are burning in the frosty air.

Is this the best way a 38-year-old father of three can earn a living? Possibly. There's nothing like bringing unexpected joy to strangers. Warming them, rubbing them together, up the wrong way – whatever it takes just to get them to somehow burst into laughter. An involuntary guffaw, a whimsical cackle and on a good night, a breathless sob.

The Grafton is a pub with a function room on top. Last time I was here, there had just been a Kosovan drug killing in the car park. Tough crowd. As I arrive the heater in the car is just beginning to clear the condensation on the windows. Fortunately the show is running late. (Shows never run early.) About 70 people are jammed into this tiny firetrap with its faded paint and peeling wallpaper. In truth most are locals from bed-sit land, glad to have a reason to be in the pub. The pay is poor, but they were one of the first clubs ever to book me and Rod is a mate. Not that I would see him socially, no thanks.

The money? Yes, that's in most people's top three questions, whether they like to ask it or not. Well there's not much logic to it – I've done gigs for everything from a fiver to five thousand – and the one for five quid was a lot harder than the other one. One-offs are better paid, but it depends on where, when and who for – but most club slots come in at a hundred or two. (Although my wife Marita and I have always measured things in 'pizzas' – one pizza equalling about £5 – well it did when I started.)

But generally comedians don't buy lottery tickets – their whole lives are complex spread bets, with hundreds and thousands being potentially won and lost every week, as gigs get cancelled or spring up at a moment's notice.

At the Grafton I bump into Steve 'Animal' Hatter. He's a comic who deals in shock, letting rip torrents of filth and abuse that invariably divide a room. A self-proclaimed wild man of comedy. He takes a call backstage – is it his drug dealer or the leader of a Satanic cult?

'No I *don't* know where your homework is!' he laughs, and then continues to hitch up his work jeans – the ones with the rips and the heavy metal badges.

There are other comics, who are exactly the same off stage as they are on, cracking gags all the time, searching for material in front of any audience. But like a full English breakfast, you don't want to face these guys every day. We are from all walks of life, except we got bored, angry or desperate and now we walk the silly walk. We were all told at one time or another 'You should be a comedian'; but most of us still doubt it every time we have a wobbly gig. We are both insecure and arrogant, for even the most humble of us effectively says through our actions – 'Let me entertain you!' Also, we all knew someone funnier than us who gave up along the way.

The Grafton gig is straightforward. A small club is always at the mercy of a group that knows each other and can intimidate the rest of the room. There's a large hen-night in, but Rod has already addressed them. They've had their moment. I even try out some new stuff about kangaroos and pickpockets which works well enough, but I'll need to try it out a few more times to hone it down to a perfect economy of words. Now to get my money, and go. Rod will pay you in coke if you want. I don't.

Right then, now it's Hemel Hempstead College. That's just round the M25. What time? – check the contract. Hitchin

College. Hitchin!? That's 30 miles up the M1! The college phones. I put my foot down, and only pull over to let a Royal Mail van past. Off the motorway, there's a minefield of rounda-bouts. Years ago towns were guarded by a wall or a moat, but these days they keep out intruders with one-way systems and directions that point the way for a while then suddenly stop without reason, so their enemies just get bored and go home. Hitchin phones again.

The compere is on stage guiding me in with his mobile. 'Does anyone here know where Dunstan Crescent is?' No. 'Apparently, Jerome, you need to do a U-turn and go back up the dual carriageway, then turn right at Homebase.'

Before I've realised it the show has passed without incident. Although I hesitate a couple of times thinking 'Have I done this bit already or was it at the last place?' Some of these kids are not that much older than my son Reg. Must stop doing these student shows before 'Dad's the entertainment'. Did 35 minutes.

Then back down the M1. At least I know the way this time. Apparently not – I still manage to get lost near Golders Green. Between shows my body is calm, but my brain is still fizzing with trial and error connections. Sleet is beginning to fall. If sleet was a comedian he could start by saying 'My mother was rain and my father was snow . . . which means . . .', no, there's nothing in that. Meanwhile the car heater is still vainly roaring against the condensation and each time I stop the whole windscreen is stained red by the brake lights of the car in front.

'What becomes of the broken hearted?'

An unusual heckle. It was two gigs ago now at the Grafton, but I've only just remembered it. What does become of them? I'll be ready for that one next time. What becomes of the broken hearted? They shout out stupid questions.

Just make it back to Leicester Square in time for the second half of the late show at the Comedy Lounge. I snaffle down a burger and fries up to 30 seconds before I go on. It used to be that I couldn't eat before a gig, this time I haven't even finished what's in my mouth. A quick look in the mirror, then I swing open the door and bound on, to punch out my stuff for the fourth and final time tonight. The energy keeps up, but I'm not sure they know why they're laughing, and I count three people asleep. There's also a party in from a pest exterminator company – rat catchers!

'I'm not talking to you' I say, 'it's probably a trap!'

Big laugh. Sometimes you think of things, sometimes you don't.

It's 2.45am and I'm crossing Trafalgar Square to find my car down by the Embankment, this time. Once again the freezing air cauterises my warm flesh. The pigeons are roosting now, turning a blind eye to those helping themselves to the Sunday papers dumped outside newsagents. There's traffic all around, the dustmen are coming and the cleaners are re-emerging from their closets.

I've just done four shows in five hours and driven over 120 miles through the labyrinth of Greater London. It's fantastic to be back to normal. Except, because of what happened recently in a faraway country, I don't think I'll ever be the same again.

Just then I run into that American open spot, who has clearly had a few drinks.

'How did it go?' I say.

'It went okay, I guess . . .'

He guesses wrong. At the late show Danny has already gleefully told me how he was booed off, and also how then, as MC, Danny had been able to use the phrase 'I'll bring the American back on!' as a way of controlling the crowd.

'Can you tell me how to get to Heathrow Airport? I've got casting in LA tomorrow.'

It may be true, but he's doing that boasting thing again. I think for a moment. 'Circle Line, that's the one you want!'

Well, that's what I would have said not so long ago. Then I'd have phoned Spaz and we'd both have snorted out loud at the thought of him doing underground laps of the capital.

Instead, I give him a lift to Hammersmith and tell him to wait for a tube.

Hidden Exit

April 2004

Yup, I would say it's about the best heckle I've ever had – being put in a prison in China. The cell's about six foot wide by eight foot long and ten feet high. Being taller than it is long, makes it feel like you're at the bottom of a well. It's damp too. There's a tiny window just beneath the ceiling. But to be honest, I've known worse dressing rooms. I'm only going to get through this ordeal if I'm grown up about it.

Oh goodie, bunk beds! The drinks from after the show are beginning to kick in. A dog barks in the distance. Prison!? I'm reminded of the film *The Shawshank Redemption* where Tim Robbins scoops his way out of his cell using only a spoon or something – must ask for any future meals to be eaten with a pneumatic drill.

Still getting laughs in my head. It's very cold in here. There's a bad smell too. But I'm already beginning to construct the anecdote in my head. So far so good, just need a funny ending now. Like, looking into the next cell and seeing someone familiar. A comic, a promoter nobody likes. No! – one of the guards recognises me from a gig in Huddersfield or somewhere – he has a word, gets me released, I sign a few photos and we all shake hands. That would be a good story.

In the meantime, sitting on the bottom bunk I try and work out what happened. After the show I'm chatting to some of the Brits.

They're friendly and seem genuinely grateful that someone has made the trip. It turns out that one of them went to my old school. His wife looks like a Chinese version of my cousin Cheryl . . . and he's telling me about corruption in local government . . . but then there's a disturbance at the back of the room. Someone's shouting in Chinese. Just then four Red Army soldiers – straight out of a Bond film as far as I can see – march up to me. An older officer is behind them, smoking a cigar.

'We take you to answer questions.'

'W-What?' I stammer, thrown by their uniforms and intensity.

'You answer questions!'

'What is it?' I recover, 'quiz night?'

But Gerry, the promoter, is getting upset.

'You can't take him. This is highly irregular, this has never happened before.'

'Take him away!'

I hear myself start a poor line about a 'Chinese takeaway' but it trails off as I'm pushed into the humid air outside. They shove me into the back of a lorry, but somehow it doesn't quite seem real. Besides I've always wanted a ride in the back of one of these trucks. It's the sort that the Vietcong would ambush American soldiers from in 'Full Metal Hamburger', or one of those films. This could still all be a wind-up. Comics often stitch each other up – Spaz had Vince Griffiths kidnapped in Croatia when they were doing shows for the troops. (Hilarious, until Vince was threatened with rape.) No, it's other comedians who get into scrapes, not me. They can disappear for days, wrestle strangers in the street or suddenly discover children they never knew they had. Not me, I've got responsibilities. Bills to pay, children I know I had.

We bounce along pot-holed roads for several miles. This is a very elaborate wind-up. I try and catch the eye of one of the guards. He's just a boy. None of them can be more than 20 years old. They're not even looking at me. Don't they know I was on ITV's *Big Talent Night*? Twice!

After about half an hour we arrive at what seems to be a police station. How bad can it be? They can torture me all they like. I'll have to turn it into a diplomatic incident. Back home there will be benefit concerts and sponsored walks. 'Release the Chinese One!' Questions will be asked in Parliament, international pressure put on the Chinese government; I could release a hostage video for Christmas. They'll never break me.

Pushed towards the door, I topple over and bash my lip on the doorpost. THAT REALLY HURT! There's blood. (Not quite as much as I think the pain deserves though.) This is real. Okay, enough, can we go back now? Bundled through several doors, the last one appears to be into a cupboard – I turn round as the door shuts; it's a cell!

It's been half an hour now. The adrenaline has gone and I'm beginning to shiver. I grab a blanket, sniff it – and throw it down again. An image of Marita and the kids all tucked up asleep appears in a balloon above my head – but I prick it with an angry stab of self-righteousness. This is not my fault. It's ridiculous. Or is it? No.

Come on, ever since I've been working as a stand-up I've always feared that one day I would get found out. Perhaps this is it – a thousand nights of travelling, performing and leaving without consequence (like a hit and run driver) have finally caught up with me. Slowly I begin to rewind my steps, to the gig, to China and right back to the beginning.

In Case Of Breakdown Stay With Vehicle

May 1993: To Torquay by coach

'Please God may the venue burn down before I get there', amen. It's only an open spot in Torquay. Five minutes, ten if it's going well – unpaid. Well, it's costing me of course. If I get away by eleven I can catch the last coach back.

It's stage time you see, like learning to be a pilot, you've got to put in the hours. But also like a pilot, one mistake can result in you plummeting to earth in a fireball. Torquay is a long way to go to be humiliated. On the other hand at least I don't know anyone who lives there – apart from Great Auntie Pauline – but she won't be dropping in by chance, not to the Bloody-Funny Club, she wouldn't stand for that! Oh yes, and she died last Christmas, I remember now.

I'm relishing every moment of this awful journey, like a condemned man who suddenly appreciates the beauty of nature on the morning of his execution. This is a lovely, fumy National Express coach, even though there's no air conditioning and the cagoule of the huge man sitting next to me is rustling constantly. We're touching. No, it doesn't matter how much I try and pull away, his immense upper arm just expands to fill the space. And he smells of chicken soup. Which reminds me I haven't eaten for 24 hours. Not sure I can do this. My palms are sweating and my stomach's churning, this isn't butterflies, there's a flock of pterodactyls under my skin.

'Business or pleasure?'

What!? Oh no, he's trying to start up a conversation! Leave me alone will you? By his accent, he's from down there in the West somewhere.

'Er, business' I say.

'Oh yes . . . ?'

'And none of yours' is what I should have said, but then for some reason the nature of my whole ghastly quest just slips out. This is because I'm still in love with the idea of being a comedian.

'Oooh' he says very impressed. 'The thing that amazes me about stand-up comedians is that they always seem to know exactly what to say.'

'Really?' I say, not knowing what to say now. (Well, a witty riposte will only mean I'll have to talk to him for the whole journey.)

I've only ever done three open spots. Two went okay and once I won a bottle of whisky in Sydenham. Not for making the 13 people in the audience laugh, you understand, but because I was the only act who wasn't booed off. We won't count Greenwich two years before: the dry mouth, the forgotten words, apologising, and then the sheep noises starting in the crowd, louder and louder. I leave the stage, the building, run home and cry into a pillow. It's a restless 18 months before plucking up the courage to book in another slot.

Each time on stage it's a duel with panic – a struggle with the twin pythons of terror and amnesia, and the more you struggle the more they squeeze. The tremor in the voice, the mistimed breath, the cloying silences, and then afterwards the shame – sympathy from maternal women, derision from older men and a wide berth from the promoter. You stick out like one of those street lamps that comes on too early. Yes, the painful truth is: the only way to get to be quite good at this is to be quite bad first.

'Hardest job in the world that, isn't it?'
  'What, oh yes, well they say so.'
  Three and a half hours of this.

The traffic is slow out of London. Going through my act in my head sometimes I forget a whole chunk for no reason. A distraction – a classic car, or a poster for underwear. Then I remember where I'm going again. My stomach turns over. Perhaps the coach will be delayed – crash, maybe! That'd be good. Not my fault. Several somersaults down a bank and into a field. I picture myself helping others to safety, becoming a hero. The Press want to talk to me; someone shoves a microphone in my face. 'Good Evening . . .', I'm on stage again and my stomach turns over once more. Over and over like a coach rolling down a hill. Just then the short-sleeved driver changes gear, lurching me out of my unhappy fantasy.

But occasionally, and just often enough, there's a 'woof' – a burst of raw energy from a crowd, enough to knock you off your train of thought, but you daren't bask in the effect of your own magic words. You soon learn to move on quickly, not to get caught in their headlights, to keep dancing in and out of the traffic of their reactions, and to save the basking for the journey home. Then there's the frustration of a line not working two shows running. What's wrong? Foxed, because a few groups of individuals are not the same as an audience – they each have their own peculiar in-jokes and loud-laughers.

It's an old coach. As the driver revs the engine, a black cloud of fumes envelops the car behind. The seats are covered with a fabric of tiny yellow, brown and red squares, ideal for concealing the stains and grime of decades. A single seat could keep a forensic scientist busy for months – countless strands of DNA, smears of hair product and the flakes of a thousand pasties.

How did I get into this? Well it was my glorious best man's speech at Ralph's wedding wasn't it? That was the thing that started this whole terrible adventure.

'I've got a lot of people to thank, but I don't want to read out a list of names in case I leave someone out or include someone who didn't help at all!' Great reviews from everyone. Yeah, several people said afterwards that I should 'turn professional'. At the time it seemed like a chance to be good at something. But it turns out that the step up to performing in front of people you don't know isn't a step, but a sheer cliff-face.

'Who are your comedy heroes then?'

He's very determined, and I hate that question. Plumbers don't have plumbing heroes do they? Pretending to be asleep – that's the only answer.

It's all my little sister's fault. She was always brilliant at everything. Super Suzy, Jerome the joker. Everyone could see it, they tell me now. Yes, if you can't compete – make a mess of things – pull a face for the camera, scribble across a birthday card, drop your trousers while doing the egg and spoon race. It made Suzy laugh as well. I've had to perform to be noticed. In the great race of life I'm definitely the one in the giant chicken costume, and not even for charity either. Yes, I'm the boy who does so badly in the high jump he has to pretend to be a limbo dancer.

The other passengers are all fascinatingly un-photogenic: from the fringes of society, too poor to afford a car or the train – students, grandparents and hapless loners down on their luck, refugees. At Victoria Coach Station other buses casually pulled up from Glasgow, Brussels and Prague all with the same sort of listless faces peering out of steamed up windows. I wish I'd arrived early now, and painted the surrounding pavements gold – just to freak them out when they stepped off the bus. But now it's our turn – a glass corridor of peasants wafting west on a cloud of soot.

'Tell us a joke then!'

'What, no sorry I'm saving all my energy for tonight.'

Why won't he leave me alone? Shouldn't have opened my eyes – that's what it was.

Cars have faces. I've always thought so. The headlamps are the eyes and the radiator or bumper is the mouth. Some look friendly and optimistic whereas others, usually depending on the angle of their headlamps, are angry and in a hurry. I'm probably an old Ford Cortina (slightly pensive); Suzy was always a Volkswagen Beetle, with a manner that put people at ease. Just as well – as a doctor, specialising in speech therapy, she's had to take on cases that others have given up on. I'm proud of her, although I could never tell her that – I have my pride, as I say. (Rather, I always told her that if she were any good she would only rely on referrals by word of mouth.) We even wrote sketches together and recorded stupid radio programmes on the tape recorders that we got for Christmas 1978.

The coach is crawling through the suburbs of London. The safe suburbs, full of bakeries, and hardware shops. I want to get off, buy a cake, and eat it with a spade. There are seagulls in town today. Perhaps it was a rough night on the coast – probably another one tonight.

We were brought up in Bexhill, Kent, and lived in the sort of suburban cherry blossom-lined avenue that's full of people learning to drive. Where clammy handed learners sit under humiliating signs like 'DOREEN' or 'BARRY' with a phone number underneath. It was a sunny childhood in a safe place, ideal for stalling, kangaroo jumps and seven point turns. It's changed a bit now – it's all residents' parking and more of an ethnic mix. But good old Mum and Dad are still there and are always keen to 'bend over backwards' if they can. I'm not sure they can so easily these days, but I'm saving that request up for a dull afternoon.

Suzy married an unbearably sensible bloke called Keith and they live in Cambridge. He has a proper job – a marketing executive for a supermarket chain, and let's just say he tends to see everything through Waitrose tinted glasses. He doesn't really get my 'humour' as he calls it, and once or twice I've looked out into an audience to see him straining at the stage as if I'm a pyramid of cut-price toilet rolls that he thinks need re-arranging. Suzy's always next to him wide-eyed and chortling, which only adds to his awkwardness. But like a property developer she has seen Keith's potential, and is slowly knocking off his corners. Well, he certainly doesn't iron his jeans as much as he used to. Suzy gets on with Marita too. Sometimes better than I do. But then she would.

I am desperate to do this, to show everyone that there's more to me than just being quiet. Yes I'm a bit shy. People don't talk about being shy these days. Well they wouldn't would they? Oh I don't want a grant, or a free parking space, but this is a real hurdle for me. Yes, I've always been scared of people, caught in the glare of their eyes, their questions having the power to jumble my brain. What *am* I doing then? Imagine my chat show. It'll be awful. Hesitation, awkward silences, guests looking at their watches.

No I can do it. To spite them all, I have chosen this mountain to climb and perhaps it will heal something inside along the way. At least if you're famous everyone gets to know you all at once, and that will surely save a thousand stilted conversations. But failure really would be misery.

At last the coach breaks the seal of the M25. Now the traffic flows freely. All around trees, grass, sheep . . . sheep noises – my stomach turns over.

Hang on, now I seem to have completely forgotten what's funny and what's not. Jokes I know work seem suddenly like random collections of words. Other observations, fuelled by adrenaline, receive standing ovations from the compliant audiences of my imagination.

Vans overtake, driven by people with real jobs. Builders, couriers, florists all employed and enjoying the ride. But, unlike comedians, no one grabs a florist by the arm after they've just finished work, looks them in the eye and says 'You're shit!'.

That's the trouble – everyone can be funny in certain situations. Everyone has felt the warmth of friends' laughter – it looks like it could be easy. But already I've learnt that finding funny words is not even half the problem. The more elusive treasure is being able to produce an atmosphere where people will laugh at them.

We pass a convoy of army vehicles. Why do they always have their lights on? Do they think we can't see them in their camouflage?

Ralph tells it like it is. He employed me one summer in his plumbing business, but come the autumn he gave me the sack. He reckoned I should get on and do the comedy thing if I was going to do it. Didn't thank him at the time, I thought it would be good to have something to fall back on. But he was right – then I *had* to make it work and it sent me all the quicker scampering up the foothills of entertainment.

Any other jobs since have just been a means to an end. Oh yes, I've known the joys of filling a skip, weeding a garden as light breaks on a freezing November morning, and licking envelopes until my tongue feels like a block of wood. Yes, I have to do this, even if for now it feels like climbing up a wet cliff-face in the dark, while wearing flip-flops.

'Do you know Ronnie Corbett?'

Cagoule man is back.

'What? Not really.'

He says he might even pop along this evening. Imagine getting no laughs at all, and all you can hear is the distant sound of a rustling mac, as he shifts impatiently from one enormous buttock to the other. He's the sort who would tell you exactly what he thought of it afterwards, too.

'Would you like some soup?' he says undoing a series of elastic bands that are holding a plastic bag around a Thermos flask.

'No thanks.'

'Hey, everyone, this lad's a comedian!'

A few other passengers turn round, and then look away incredulously.

Then he shouts into his soup. 'But I've been sat here for two hours and I haven't laughed once!'

A few of them half-smile.

He gives me a cheeky sideways grin, but now he's got soup on his beard. Hope it's soup.

I could always kill him. That would get me out of tonight. They'd have to stop the bus, call the police. The trial would grip the nation. But then what if, when I took the stand, I made the jury laugh? Then I'd never forgive myself.

Prison 1

Shanghai is unfinished. Skyscrapers spring up like bean-shoots into the smog that rises from huge twisting double-storey freeways, which carry a constant flow of taxis, vans and bicycles. The sky seems permanently overcast, as if it's given up putting on a show for a disinterested city.

Sure, we all know about China – China and India – how well they're doing, what a great future they have – like successful cousins your Mum goes on about. Resident associations don't seem to hold much sway here, and using a horn isn't exactly a last resort either, but simply means 'Hello I've got a car'. Mopeds join in with more flatulent notes. Oh, and it all smells of a mixture of noodles and urine.

A few years ago no one really drank coffee here. Now there's a Starbucks on nearly every corner. But the place is both familiar and alien in equal measure. There are ancient backstreets – an unplanned hash of pagoda curves and corrugated shacks, all soaked for centuries in wood smoke and spices. The sudden hiss of a wok, the flutter of a nervous pigeon, the crunching of gears in an old man's throat as he hawks onto the pavement. On the other hand, the clouds, office blocks and the department stores are pretty much the same as Luton. But I suppose what impresses me most is that there are so many Chinese, and also how difficult it is to grasp how many thoughts, words, meals and lives have all gone before, and none of them with any reference to me, or anyone I know.

Two shows at The Carnaby Street, an ex-pat pub in the old part of town. A watering hole for swapping gossip and watching live English football – all within a vast foreign desert. It's an outpost of home more British than Britain. The Queen's portrait hangs on the wall next to a poster for a St George's Day Disco. The staff are all Chinese of course, and I wonder what they make of it – the equal pride and disdain with which ex-pats celebrate their culture. Also I wonder how they feel about local teenage girls who couple themselves with middle-aged Western men? How would the lads of Essex react, for instance, if all the town's top tottie disappeared off on the arms of rich Chinese businessmen?

We're here for less than a week. There's a gig, then three days off before another one in a different part of town. (Six days is usually about the right amount I find, before me and my stomach start to complain.)

I'm here with Arnie Zoot a bachelor who doesn't like foreign food, or get up before noon. (Why did he come?) Like many comics he doesn't drink either. Not because he never did, but because he's been there, done that, stained the T-shirt. He's also a fairly stereotypical Australian, which is probably a harder habit to kick, although it would be interesting to see if he could go 'cold turkey' for a week – you know, only whispering, and never mentioning how much sunnier it is where he comes from.

His act is a slick and cheery description of the differences between men and women. He expertly plays the sexes off against each other soliciting shrieks and jeers in equal measure. He's good company, when he's awake, but for the most part I'm sightseeing on my own.

On Monday, I visit a market downtown. There are pitiful stalls displaying a few mouldy vegetables and the odd scrawny chicken. I walk into one shack to see what's in three red plastic bowls at the back. Nothing – it's the bowls that are for sale. There's a stale warm smell like a half-remembered school dinner. Now a middle-aged man is smiling and his wife is tugging at my sleeve. 'Special price' she bleats. Why would I want three red plastic bowls?

Just then, I'm saved as Gerry the promoter rings. A gig's come up in Guangdong Province, tomorrow – somewhere beginning with

'X'. it's a few hours away by plane – for some oil-workers, pay's okay, and I'd be back in time for the weekend show in Shanghai. He'll come with me. Do I fancy it? Why not?

That afternoon it's back to the airport and onto the sort of internal flight that goes missing, and then only makes about fifth or sixth item on the BBC News. I'm the only person on the plane with brown hair, which will at least make identification of the body slightly easier.

'X' turns out to be like Shanghai but without the fresh air. There's plenty of building going on here too, mostly in collaboration with Western companies. The engineers and architects employed by the oil company to build a refinery are desperate for anything that sounds like home. I oblige, and even the mention of 'Marmite' gets a cheer. Not a standing ovation exactly but at the end many of them clapped with their hands above their heads.

Then it all kicked off. Gerry had mentioned that the not-so-secret police often sit in. (They're the only nationals who aren't behind the bar.)

36 bricks high, 18 bricks long. The other side is 13 wide and 32 high. (The inaccessible window accounting for the spare four bricks.) On one side there's a thin shelf. What for? The door is metal and cold to the touch.

There's no writing on the wall by previous prisoners. I thought you were supposed to score off the days in bunches of five or is that only in cartoons? Perhaps nobody's been in here longer than a day. Or no previous occupant has been able to write – illiterate, or too badly beaten up. I'll record the hours. That should throw any future archeologist. Two already.

I've spent years in this job trying to place myself in the right place at the right time, but it turns out the wrong place at the wrong time has come up first. Suddenly what I do for a living seems very light and frivolous. Stupid, even.

Just then I remember Gerry explaining how they deal with petty criminals round here. The thief is put on the back of a lorry, surrounded by soldiers and then driven back to the scene of the crime. After everyone's had a good look they're driven off and never seen again. Perhaps I'll be taken back to the venue, and then taken out and shot for using too many puns. Fair enough.

Uneven Surface

September 1993: Cherbourg to
Portsmouth by ferry

I love my wife. We're on a ferry in the middle of a storm in the English Channel and she is cleaning up our children's sick. At this moment it's she who's holding us all together. We're coming home two days early from our camping trip because of persistent rain. Marita deals with each child patiently in turn, corralling them with her arms and soothing voice. Her delicate features are encircled with the red string of the anorak, like a job ringed with a pen in a newspaper.

I'm glad I chose her. Why she sticks with me, sometimes I'm not so sure. I'm wearing a green anorak to go with my face. Well, it was a pleasant day in Cherbourg this morning when it seemed like a good idea to buy a large box of cakes and scoff the lot while waiting in the queue for the boat. I would happily protect my family from any other enemy, men with guns or dogs with rabies, but nausea has me undone.

This is fairly typical. I'm the one with the big ideas who wants to have his own TV show, but I have no sense of direction and trouble tying my own shoe laces. Marita is the practical one. Another more profound example of my ineptitude is that I've managed to choose the fields and beaches of Normandy for this happy family trip, somehow forgetting that my wife is German! Nevertheless, I try and lighten things up.

'Just a couple more hours of this.'
'Five!'
'Five?'
'Cherbourg to Portsmouth is five hours.'
'Why?'
'It's further.'
'Is it?'
'You said it would save us driving.'

The Princess of Portsmouth is full of large lorries with foreign number plates and cars with GB stickers and roof racks – a huge amount of metal to be carried on the water. We have a Ford Sierra estate (unfussy but useful). Reg and Stan are three and one years old, and keen to stay on deck for the whole journey, but they both seem small enough to slip through the rails at any moment.

Fifty years on, Normandy is still scarred by the effects of World War II – museums, memorials and cemeteries. Seeing the thousands and thousands of white tombstones lined up affected Marita deeply. I was brought up on war films and comics but the sheer horror of it all is beginning to get through to me now. Besides, we have boys, and if we bothered to look at the names chiselled on the graves, no doubt it wouldn't take us long to find a Stan, or a Reg.

In our own tiny way we too have been struggling with the idea of sacrifice – we're still fighting the Battle of the Bottle, but mercifully, for the moment, all is quiet on the Wetting the Bed Front. It's a thankless task and we would happily lay a wreath at the tomb of the Unknown Parent, had we the energy. Plenty of other comics I know seem to live the life of a well-paid student with just a few bursts of extraordinary concentration. They get up at noon and generally behave like sociable but unwise owls, staying up all night and then trying to trick prey into coming back to their nest.

'Daddy why is the sea green?'
'Because it reflects the sky.'
'But the sky isn't green!'

Reg is at an age where he asks questions all the time. I don't know why, and I'm not going to ask.

'Come and read a book with Mutti.'
'Why is Daddy lying down?' Reg asks her.
'Daddy's tired.'
'Why?'
'Because he works hard.'
'No he doesn't.'

We met in 1989 when the Berlin Wall came down. Well, I'd heard that girls from the East were coming over and kissing boys they didn't even know! So Ralph and I immediately got on a coach to Germany and then stood around hopefully at the Brandenburg Gate. Marita was the first girl I met.

Now, when women hear this they often seem to think it's one of the most romantic things they've ever heard. So, I'm always quick to point out to any bilious looking bloke beside them, that Marita was actually a West German tourist coming back from a day out. Also, that she'd already spent six months in St Albans, England working as an au pair and that at the time she was engaged to a Bavarian ski instructor. But even so, I knew there was something special about her, and it wasn't just her bleached blonde hair, her funky red leather jacket or the way her big blue eyes seemed to transcend the need for any kind of translation. (Admittedly her perfect English helped with this too.)

Actually nothing more might have come of it, except for our other reason for being there – to buy and drive home one of those iconic East German cars, a Trabant (stylishly foreign). Then, when we got home Ralph was going to do it up and sell it for a huge profit. Eventually we bought one for cash in Leipzig but then it blew up 70 kilometres down the autobahn. Our mechanic's detailed technical report then concluded that now it was just 'a piece of crap' and we were stranded.

'I'll phone Marita' I said.
'What, the girl with the miniskirt?' said Ralph.
'Did she have a miniskirt? I didn't notice.'
'Course you didn't.'

We ended up staying at her place for three days. Then she

came to visit me at college in England, and the rest is history. Well, history and geography. There was a lot of driving and flying and meeting halfway involved. But in those days miles covered just fuelled our exotic passion. Two years later we were married and had set up home in a rented flat in West London.

Stan is now fast asleep in the double buggy. The pushchair is made by Maclaren. Not the same company who make racing cars surely? I picture myself sprinting the boys past a chequered flag. The crowd go wild, except Marita who is pointing to an empty seat. Stan must have fallen out at the last chicane.

In time it became apparent that my wife had a terrible secret. A filthy horrible ambition that some find too much to cope with. She wants to be a housewife. That's her ambition. Not a housewife who hangs up her trouser suits for a couple of years and brings up children as if she's running a small PR company. No, her stated long-term goal is to stay at home, look after the kids and run the house. An unreconstructed man's dream perhaps, but only if you have a job and your pride intact.

In the meantime she works part time for that PR company, sometimes through the night to meet deadlines, to make sure there's food on the table, and I, well, I eat it. They should give her the account for motherhood and childbirth – she could turn it round like someone did with Marks and Spencer. After all her first words after giving birth to Reg were 'didn't hurt so much'.

As I lie face down in the sweaty red vinyl of the seats of the indoor viewing deck, I can hear the echoes of chirpy banter amongst the crew. They have strange titles like 'petty officer' and 'purser'. Growing up in Portsmouth did they dream of commuting to the continent every day and wiping tables with wooden edges to contain the spills? Or did they just fail the Navy exam? This is a familiar position for me, trying to catch a few seconds' sleep face-down on the sofa, protecting myself, before the boys mistake me for a human trampoline again.

never gives the order to 'abandon train'. You do get abandoned cars though.

No, I'm in this for the long haul. But will it always be like this? Lots of people give up, decide it's not for them, and go into writing, teaching or denial. Maybe they're the strong ones. Maybe it's all just a fascination with the edge of a precipice. The intoxication of being so close to either, a death plunge or soaring up into the clouds carried by the goodwill of strangers.

On holiday, it's taken me about a week to begin to relax, but yesterday my stomach involuntarily turned over when Reg handed me his dripping ice cream cone, and my hand took on the shape of holding a microphone.

The boat creaks. The horizon disappears again.

'Daddy can I have another cake?'

'What!?'

'I'm hungry.'

'But you've just been sick.'

'But I'm hungry again now.'

'Let's just wait till we get to the land.'

'When will that be?'

'In a few hours.'

'How many hours?'

'Just under five.'

'You said it would be two hours.'

No, the bug has bitten. I've had just enough good nights to know that this is all I want to do. To make people laugh, and as many as possible. I've felt that huge fraternal energy that soars to climax after climax. It starts with words but then goes far beyond as, just for a second, everyone shares the moment, as you suddenly shine a torch on a previously hidden thought or image.

I will suffer the training and make it work. It's just that you've got to do all your learning in public – that's what's so hard. In a 20-minute set that's 60 to 80 cast iron laughs, and it's not good enough to be simply engaging or amusing, you have to be laugh-out-loud-funny the whole time. I will succeed.

But last night I had a disturbing dream. I was on a jumbo jet with all my family and friends, when a voice came over the tannoy saying that rebels were surrounding the airport – and was there anyone who knew how to fly the plane? I stood up and told everyone to relax. Looking a bit surprised, they all broke out into spontaneous applause and gave me high fives all the way to the cockpit. Then I started the plane up, took off and flew it straight into the side of a mountain.

Sorry For Any Delay

January 1994: Tube from London

Tonight I got paid for making people laugh! Not in beer or rotten fruit – cash! One ten-pound note and a five. (Three pizzas.) Yes, people paid money for me to make them laugh. Me!

Several stops have passed, but I'm lost in the wonder of an ambition achieved. Just check the money's still there. It's not! Oh yes, I bought a round of drinks afterwards, there are just a few coins left – but that's not the point. Opposite are other professionals coming home after doing what they do. I've just done what I do too, oh yes baby. I loll back and drink in the atmosphere. I've worked hard for this. So I *can* do it after all. Ha ha – here we go!

I'll recall this moment in a documentary one day. A retrospective of a comedy great, wandering round my vineyard in Tuscany with Melvyn Bragg.

'Tell us about the moment you knew that you were going to be a great comedian . . .'

I'll smile wryly and then bending down pluck a leaf off a vine. 'You know Melvyn, making comedy is like making a good wine . . .'

'Really?'

'It takes a while . . . and then people like it.'

Melvyn just stares at me. The noise of crickets in the background. Not sure what to do now. So I push him over.

Some of them have been working late; others have been at shows in the West End or drinking after work. A businessman is asleep opposite. That could be me in a dull job. Can't he see the dead end he's in? Three girls, secretaries probably, are laughing loudly at the other end of the carriage. Sounds familiar, of course, I make people laugh for a living! – did I mention that? Perhaps I should go over and do a few minutes – no, better not, we don't want any of them to pass out do we?

My first paid gig had just crept up on me. I'd been doing a lot of open spots recently and then there was a pull-out at the Lavender Tree in Baker Street. £15 for 10 minutes. It wasn't even a tough show. It's just a small room above a pub, and I'd met a couple of the acts before and this helps put me at ease. The bigger venues are more frightening, with huge crowds, professional promoters, acts who do it full time – people you've seen off the telly – a club within a club. But this are a friendly crowd – all 33 of them. (Okay, when a party of seven left at the interval it caused a bit of a dent, but I needn't have worried.) What a crowd the rest were! How many people in this carriage? Twenty-six. Yes, I could easily reprise my set. I pick up a newspaper but the words won't go in. Life is good.

Those Canadian girls invited me to come and have a drink with them afterwards, but I declined. The look in their boyfriends' eyes swung it.

Stop at Earls Court where a lot of people change. The engine lets out more air. What has it been eating? Figs?! The doors roll almost shut, but I leap up to hold them open for a bloke with a rucksack. A fellow human being. He nods. I say 'thanks'. (It shouldn't be that way round should it? It doesn't matter.)

Back to the documentary: a blue plaque on the wall outside the Lavender Tree, some grainy footage of me doing stand-up on TV, then a montage of my roles in various classic sitcoms, yes, and then that scene from the film that won me my first Oscar. Melvyn interjects:

'I read somewhere that scene was entirely improvised. Is that true?'

'Yes it was Melvyn. Scorsese was always encouraging me just to go for it, and you know, to see if Brad could keep up.'

Marita wanted to come. 'Wait till I do a bigger show' I said, meaning 'Wait till I'm sure I won't die'. Wish she had come now. That all my friends and relatives were there. I wish I'd handed out leaflets in the street to passers-by. Perhaps there were agents or film producers in the audience! Didn't have weeks to get nervous for this one, no, I just got up and did it. There were a few anxious moments, standing at the back trying to get a measure of the crowd, like a sailor reading the sea – after all I was going to have to walk on it.

Going through my act again, and I can hear almost the exact response for each line. Admittedly I got a bigger laugh from an improvised question, than from any of my rehearsed material.

'Where do you live?' I said.

'Iran' he said.

'Is that on the Northern line?'

There were hoots of laughter. Hoots I tell you. Perhaps next time I should just ask each person where they're from. Then when they answer I could say things like 'Is that on the Piccadilly line, Jubilee etc'. It could be my catchphrase. The name of my Las Vegas show could be – 'Is that on the Bakerloo?'.

Mustn't get carried away. But it's a magical feeling – putting yourself in danger, and then saving yourself before their very eyes. It's all about living through that moment of fear isn't it? That tiny moment of perfect terror between punch-line and response, arrow and target, jump and bungee.

Terry Machin, the MC, was fantastic. Standing there, sweating in his union jack waistcoat. I suppose comics feel safe because he's not difficult to follow, and, in brutal terms, if the leopard turns at least there's one person in the room who can't run as fast as you can. Although it's a different skill being a compere. You have to be the audience's mate and, on a difficult night, you have to pipe smoke into the wasps' nest. And of course if they don't like you, you still have to face them again and again and again.

First up had been Lloyd Pritchard. He's very experienced. Good, too. Blokey observations, dipping in and out of the crowd, smiling, making it look easy. Imperious actually. In truth my only misgiving is that if he was really any good he should be famous by now, surely? He's in his mid forties, I almost feel sorry for him, but he's very nice to me.

My slot's in the middle. Ideal – the audience are warmed up but not tired. I throw caution to the wind and give it my best, and I win. Some people cheer, as well as clap as I leave the stage. Shame you don't get the chance to really enjoy people laughing, you always have to be thinking of the next thing. But I can hear them now in my head. Some laughs are like a car that won't start, the engine turning over and gradually running out of breath. Others are long and elongated like a screaming man continually falling off a cliff. I think my favourite is the one that sounds like a mouse inflated with helium, that's suddenly let go and flies around the room.

Twenty-six people, at, what, four laughs a minute (at least), for ten minutes that's, well you do the maths . . . please. I don't have to, that's not my job.

Before every show I feel the need to clear my conscience. Like a soldier attending mass before going over the top. Tonight with minutes to spare I phoned Marita to apologise for not listening to her today. (She had then asked me how I knew I hadn't listened – I'll being sorting that one out later.) But afterwards you forget the pain of just before.

There can't be many jobs where you are just employed to make people physically react – osteopaths, prostitutes, ghost train owners . . . .

I half smile at an elderly couple opposite who are studying the programme for the musical *Cats*. I'm in show business. I wonder if they can tell.

Hang on, fifteen pounds for ten minutes, that's ninety pounds per hour. For an eight-hour day that's . . . seven hundred and twenty pounds per day!

Fast forward: putting my hands in concrete on Hollywood Boulevard. Receiving a hero's welcome at Heathrow along with the Beatles, who've magically re-formed.

A stadium full of screaming fans. A helicopter lands on the pitch. I climb up on to the stage.

'Good evening Wembley!'

The crowd goes crazy. Some girls are on the shoulders of their disgruntled boyfriends. They're waving at me.

'Tell me, is Wembley on the Central line?'

Now even some of the St John's Ambulance Brigade are becoming hysterical.

I get it now. What a magical art form! And it's entirely self-regulating. The audience only laughs at what's funny. Like a self-cleaning oven, the dross is burned up. Not like theatre or fine art where people can make a living based on pretentious cobblers.

Fifteen quid is a start. Not that there's much of it left, and, thinking about it, I haven't got any other paid gigs coming up. An historic night though, and worth celebrating.

Gunnersbury! I've missed my stop! Who cares, I'm a professional comedian, all sorts of madcap things happen to me. Gunnersbury – is that on the District Line? Yes, yes it is.

Prison II

So a thousand journeys later here I am. It's as if I've fallen asleep, missed my stop and then woken up at the end of the line. But I'm not the same person now. I'm, older, wiser, stronger . . . heavier. My embryonic career is now a hard-boiled egg.

Listen, I can hear a drip! It's just like one on a sound effects tape. In fact that's almost the exact effect you would use if you wanted to recreate the sound of a cell in a Chinese prison, on the radio or in a film. But films don't smell this bad. Or take this long. We'd cut back to an anxious girlfriend, or to an SAS team planning a rescue mission. Then we'd see the guards playing cards or Mah-jong or something. Chinese Monopoly, where everything is owned by the state. One of them would pick up a 'Get out of Jail Free' card and they'd all laugh a bit too loud and long.

'Oi!' I shout. 'Oi!' There's a small echo. And then silence. That worked then. Shall I demand to see my lawyer? That's what you're supposed to do isn't it? I have a feeling I may as well demand to see Lord Lucan. Perhaps this is where he is. Along with Elvis, the Loch Ness Monster . . . and the remote control for the television.

I am entirely innocent aren't I? I am. Unless they plant something on me. Weapons, drugs, rhododendrons. I wonder if I could survive torture? Why would they torture me? Perhaps they've seen my act.

'Oi! Oi! . . . Oiiiiii!'

No one's listening. I have no audience now. No need to panic, have a panic attack. Or worry about having a panic attack. But this isn't funny anymore. Here, I could get ill. Ill or shot. I swallow.

A gulp, like in a cartoon. Like when Bugs Bunny is looking down the barrel of a shotgun. I've been in tight spots before. Silence. Not this far from home though. Gulp, again.

That drip could get quite annoying.

Emergency Exit

October 1994: Train from Lime Street
to London

There was a time when I used to like the North of England, but that was 24 hours ago now, and just before I arrived. Then everyone was friendly, down to earth and the Arctic wind was merely refreshing. Now the breeze definitely seems more hostile and cuts through me not so much like a knife, more a sharpened spoon – gently prodding and scraping, just enough to put off anyone who's not sure they should be here.

I'm supposed to have done two gigs in Liverpool but now, after having done just one of them, I'm running down the platform to catch a train back to London. Leaping aboard, I collapse into a seat and begin to sweat. The train pulls out far too slowly. We pass the backs of some big old houses. Then a lumber yard. Over there, there's another train with a few broken windows, in a siding, going nowhere. That's my career that is.

Of course I'd heard that it can be difficult to entertain people up here. That they think *they're* the funny ones, either that or they seem to know someone called 'Our Jimmy' who could have you in stitches by just raising an eyebrow at four hundred yards. So before the first show I'm more nervous than usual. I'm also preceded by a couple of local acts who make references to certain shops and housing estates, that bring knowing chuckles and applause, but of course I've no idea what they're talking about.

At least I'm experienced enough to know that playing the 'outsider' card is the best way to win them over. And it works! It's true that there are a few heckles – and that they're the sort of heckles that an effete Southerner has no hope of understanding, but I just ask for subtitles and they at least seem to appreciate my fighting spirit. Yes, they're a sporting crowd – the sort who either really like you or really don't, and I quit while I'm ahead.

Rex, the owner of the nightclub, takes me into his office after the show. In the main room next door the disco has started, and one of Kylie's bass lines is thumping through the wall. The office is damp, with a dirty computer in the corner, which is balanced on top of boxes full of industrial-sized ketchup containers.

Rex is tall with stubble, and a green silk open neck shirt – all cufflinks and eyelashes, a man for the ladies and he even coughs with a Scouse accent. He jokes with Pat the bouncer who then shakes my hand. Pat has enormous hands – imagine 10 large uncooked sausages, three with sovereign rings. His chubby fingers and big, bald head remind me of Stan as a baby, but I won't mention that. His boss, Rex, like many people who run clubs is a frustrated performer. He certainly has the charm, but probably not the desperate single mindedness necessary to keep on getting up in front of an audience. He is funny though. I've laughed out loud three times in the last minute. The accent seems to help – it makes everything seem like a question to which the answer is a laugh. Pat has some jokes he wants to tell me too, but I can already guess from the naughty glint in his eye that they're probably going to be horribly racist. Quickly I ask him how long he's lived in Liverpool.

'Ay, I'm a Manc!' he growls as if I've just spat in his dinner. Ah, now I know a little bit about this. There's the north-south divide obviously, and then there's the north-north west divide, as in the War of the Roses etcetera. But far more vicious than either of those is the north west-north north west divide. Yes,

Pat was born just 20 miles away in Manchester but it might as well be Manchuria.

'Oh, are you a United fan?' I offer.

'City till I die!'

And then of course there's the great Manchester divide.

Rex saves the moment. 'We'll just add up the money, then give you a lift back to the hotel', he says with a flashing smile.

'Thanks' I say, relieved.

Looking round I see a laminated Safety at Work notice curling off the wall. It gives a list of exactly how long you can keep raw meat in the fridge.

In the next room the disco is in full swing. There are whoops and screams and occasionally the DJ turns off the music and the audience sing-in the gaps. Plumbers don't do that – as you watch them work, suddenly down tools and leave a bit of the pipe for you to fix.

Then in comes Haydee – the girl on the door, who'd kissed me on the cheek and we'd never even met. Perhaps she'd just seen my publicity photo and thinks she knows me. But now, of course, she's raised the stakes too high and we'll have to make awkward lunges at each other every time we meet. Who knows, the whole thing might spiral out of control – a kind word here, a misunderstood syllable there – and before you know it I could be at a registry office – a bigamist before you can say 'our Jack Robinson'.

'You alright chuck?'

'Er yeah, fine thanks. How are you?'

Then I hear all about her evening – an argument with a difficult group of punters, a conversation with someone called Leslie, her Mum's hip operation, the corns she has from wearing new shoes. She must be in her early twenties and seems to have seen a little more of a sun-bed than is healthy. She's also wearing orange lipstick, which makes her look as if she's always just finished a large bowl of spaghetti bolognaise.

'We've just got to count up the money then we'll give you a lift back' she says.

'Great.'

I wonder how many people are coming on this trip back to the hotel?

I think I've met other 'Haydees' before – vulnerable but tactile, devaluing the currency of touch, by flooding the market with hugs – as popular with men as she is unpopular with her own sex.

Suddenly, outside, there are raised voices and the sound of splintering wood. Instinctively I recognise the 'wumph' of fist on human flesh. I freeze for a second, and then put my head round the door. Pat is kicking a thin bloke with a beard down the stairs. (Perhaps that's why they call them 'punters'?) Some of the bloke's hippy friends are protesting, but they settle for being able to leave with his damaged body, like disciples scuttling from the Cross. Pat now stands at the entrance panting like a bulldog, and then he wipes his brow with a pink handkerchief. That's a bit camp I think. But I don't think I'll mention this either.

Rex drives an old Jaguar, sleek and intent like its driver. He chats away to Haydee in the front beside him. Tuning in to their conversation from the back, I suddenly realise that she's actually called Heidi, and it's just the way they say it. Hurriedly, I review my mental CCTV tapes of the evening to make sure I haven't called her anything too strange.

Just then we stop at some tenements and a youth in a baseball cap appears out of the shadows. Rex gives him a package wrapped in brown paper. I don't like this; I don't like this at all. Perhaps I should say something, interrupt with a song from a musical or a raucous King Kong impression – yes, you often hear of drug deals 'going wrong', but that's probably not what they mean is it?

'Ay tell Mam I had to get smoky bacon' says Rex.

My mistake – it's just someone's supper. The youth takes it and disappears. In the circumstances a King Kong impression would've been difficult to explain. Although if it had been drugs, being arrested and ending up with a criminal record wouldn't be bad, as far as my career as a comedian is concerned. It might just help mark me out as a crazy renegade who pays no attention to society's rules. Well, certainly more than having a wife and children and living in Ealing does.

Eventually we get to Haydee/Heidi's block. She kisses everyone goodnight in turn, then gets out and wanders into the gloom towards a graffiti covered stairwell.

'Poor kid' says Rex as he swerves the car round and turns up some sort of classical music. He's full of surprises.

'I think Pat might have been smackin' er about a bit' he says concerned.

'Pat the bouncer's been hitting her?' I say.

'Yeah.'

Then I laugh. Rex gives me a look. Why did I laugh?! That was the last thing I meant to do. I think it was just the way he said 'yeah'. I am so out of my depth here.

My 'hotel' is the basement of a large guesthouse. The room is warm and everything has a crocheted cover. The bed, the television, the toilet-roll holder and even the landlady, come to think of it. The combined effect of décor and humidity makes it feel as if you've got flu in Brazil in the 1950s. There are also metal bars on the windows in case anyone tries to steal any of the valuable knitted work, and the toilet smells as if it's always just been vacated by a large horse. In the early hours I lie on top of the bed in my clothes, not able to bring myself to put bare flesh against the bobbly nylon sheets. Eventually I fall asleep overcome with the chloroform-like cocktail of damp and warmth.

Back on the train we rip through a station like a zip up a cardigan. It hurts my eyes to try and read the name on the signs as we shoot past, but I keep trying, not wanting to be beaten. Runcorn!

I spend the next morning watching the fuzzy television and walking round the shops. It's a crisp winter's day and the sun is shining. The granite towers and stone wharves have been turned into offices and cafés now, emasculated, like old soldiers at a tea party. But everyone's out, pleased to see each other and taking the time to stop and talk. That doesn't happen in London, well only if there's been some kind of fatal incident, that's stopping us getting where we're going.

I want to join in but I'm not sure how. As I turn a corner there's a man sitting on the pavement staring vacantly in front of him. As I pass, I drop 50p into his cup.

'Ay that's me coffee!'

I offer to buy him another, but I don't seem to have any change – well, not anymore.

Eventually I find my way to Heidi's block, where Rex has arranged to pick me up. I'm there a few minutes early, and she calls down to me from about five floors up, and then I zigzag into the mist up the wrought iron stairs.

Baring her wrists towards me, she throws her arms around my neck, but I feel a little more relaxed, now that I've seen her do this to everyone. Besides now I feel sorry for her.

'Alright chuck, I've just put the kettle on.'

She's sniffling, and there's a red mark above her eye. I don't have to ask, it all tumbles out – Pat came round last night, he was drunk. There was a fight – the neighbours called the police, she went to her Mum's. She's only just got back and her uncle has changed the locks. Then she asks what I think she should do. Me? I don't know. What should I say? Move to Japan? Become a nun?

'Dump him!' I say, my empathy falling out rather abruptly. 'Yeah, teach the fat ox a lesson!'

She laughs, but for some reason this feels like I've stepped over a line. Of course, she probably even loves him doesn't she?

There's a bit of a gap and then the Citizens' Advice Bureau is my next best soft Southern suggestion. Then I go on to patron-isingly explain what it does.

'Oh yeah they're on the High Street' she says bending over a pile of washing, revealing a black lacy thong. For a second, it looks like an elaborate eye-patch she might have horribly misunderstood. I begin to hum, to cover the sudden halt in conversation. (I never hum.)

'Do you know, I like talking to you, you seem like a good listener' she says.

'Pardon!?'

'You seem like a good listener.'

'No, I was joking. You said I was a good listener, and I said pardon.'

'Oh. I see. You were so funny last night as well.'

She's still being far more friendly than necessary, but, I'm married and she's . . . orange.

Just then a baby cries in another room. A baby?

'Alright Shelley.'

I picture a baby in a shell suit. Or perhaps covered in seashells – daughter of Neptune god of the Sea. Heidi brings her in. She's a nice looking kid, and her Mum carries on to me chatting as if I've known her all her life. Perhaps I've been wrong about Heidi.

She's asking my advice on security now – like I would know. 'I'm gonna sleep with an 'ammer under my pilla.'

'Good idea' I say.

Then to show willing, I begin to check the locks on the windows. I continue on round, until I come to the larder. But there's something large on the floor towards the back. Is it some sort of sack? No it's warm and breathing and all at once it lurches forward.

'Pat!'

I keep re-living this moment on the train. Each time I remember it I squirm in my seat. Why are we spending so long in Stoke? If Rex gives Pat a lift in his Jag they could catch us up!

I don't remember actually running down the fire escape, but I do remember how it shuddered the moment Pat put one of his ox-like hooves on it, two flights above me. I'd flown out of the flat, pulling a chair across his path, which slowed him down vitally. So he was there the whole time! As I run across the yard beneath him, he hangs over the rail and screams something bestial, something from the very back of his throat, a guttural Northern curse encased in phlegm, the gist of which is to go away and not to come back for a very long time indeed. And do you know, I think I'm probably going to take this citizen's advice.

Prison III

No escape here though. Haven't sat this still for . . . about 10 years now. I've always had gigs to do, jokes to write, nappies to change. Always moving on. It's not unusual to drive to somewhere like Leicester, stay two hours – then come back again. Yeah, I could have driven to Sheffield by now, Ipswich maybe.

Sometimes comedians are more paid drivers than performers. Tired for a decade. It used to be I could never nap, but having children came with one consolation super-power – being able to nod off at a moment's notice. Both of us – Narcolepsy Man and his flagging assistant Catnap Woman. Even when I'm awake there's often a tiny circle of my vision rotating like an extractor fan. Or a headache that's on hold, to have properly when I have a moment. A life lived on the edge of nausea kept in check by regular injections of adrenaline.

I decorated a bathroom about this size once, when I was doing odd jobs years ago. Magnolia and white. Getting dust and brush hairs caught in the gloss. I've come a long way since then. But now I'm tired and cold, and I want to go home. Not just to Shanghai but back to West London. To familiar suburbs where I know what the rules are: to leafy streets that, in the summer, shimmer with the smoky essence of barbecues. Where tree-lined avenues and crescents curl round each other like snakes in a pet shop window.

But the quaint roads of England seem thousands of miles away now – probably because they *are* thousands of miles away. Don't even know where I am – X- something. X marks the spot, but there's no buried treasure here. Just a big mistake.

I sneeze, but it has a 'poor me' inflexion – emphasis on the 'choo'. No one to say 'Bless you' either.

This telling jokes business has got out of hand. I was only kidding. Yes, it's as if I've met the rough boys in the park and now I'd quite like to go home for tea, please.

London 100

There's a big black man trying to get into the boot of my car! In a performance situation I'm learning to control my body, but this little surprise has me frozen in rubbery fright. Shouting at him from the edge of the dimly lit car park, I want my voice to sound like an angry Robert de Niro, but instead it just comes out like Yogi Bear.

'Hey, what are you doin'?' (Boo Boo)

He looks up, then walks round to the front of the car, or rather to the boot of the car in front, and opens it. His car is the same make, model and colour as mine.

'Sorry mate, wrong car' he mutters.

Just as well I didn't get my retaliation in first. It's like something out of a Race Relations film. I get in and start the engine, stall, and then charge off – I'll do my seat belt up later.

Usually the further you travel the more pleased they are to see you. Unless of course you're two hours late and the headliner has had to go on before you. Well, getting to Norwich from West London takes longer than you think. Once you get off the motorway you've got A and B roads all the way until just outside Holland. (Don't people come for their holidays on the Norfolk Broads?)

Lennie Parks, the headliner, was very nice about it actually. He's an ageing hippie with a toothy smile, a natural storyteller who cajoles the audience with charm-laced intellect, 'Hooray I'm Alive Comedy' – a celebration of inadequacy, and I genuinely regret missing it. He's one of the acts I used to watch before I started, but now I get to share the same dressing room and call him 'Lennie' myself. But he's always very encouraging, unlike some other established comics who are more keen to see if I can cut it, before letting me into their circle.

If he has a weakness, it's going on too long, but that's worked in my favour tonight. He'd have been able to turn the whole black-man-boot-of-car incident into half an hour of acerbic social comment. Someone said he was once offered his own TV show but turned it down because he didn't want to become too famous. Why? I guess he could never be doing with all the photo-shoots and chat shows necessary to go up to the next level, he doesn't even own a mobile phone for goodness sake.

The milometer says 79982. Must watch out for 80000. Why? Don't know. Well it's a milestone, isn't it? Like a birthday for a car. Although like people over a certain age, I suppose it just means you're that much nearer being broken up for parts.

Lennie was more at home when the circuit was run on more socialist lines, when Thatcherism was the enemy and acts got paid the same genuine door-split. But then comedy got Thatchered itself, and the evil Empire bought off the rebels with cash and TV shows. Lennie doesn't trust telly, it's not what he signed up for, it's a sellout. Well, it's certainly what killed live comedy in the States – too much weak stand-up on the box meant no one went to see it live anymore. Now many of them are over here.

Lennie has seen the arrival of a new breed of comic, technically proficient but with nothing much to say – clowns not prophets. Blokes who just talk about themselves, or who re-hash what you've heard someone else do before. Kids not long out of university with no real life experience who can only digress into articulate whimsy about goblins and nonsense. Now the alternative is mainstream, and the only politics comedians seem angry about is the politics of their own industry – who's getting what and whether they deserve it.

I don't want to play the game either. Never did. At school I remember not wanting to put my hand up, to answer questions, because it was clear the teachers already knew the answers. It felt like a mild form of abuse. But couldn't Lennie use the system against itself? Have his own subversive TV show? That's what I want to do. Speak to the nation on my own terms.

Stopped at the lights: in the mirror, I notice that the two people in the car behind are fighting! No, it's just one man putting his coat on. Still on edge, and my thoughts are nervously flitting about.

Yes, Lennie was more at home in the mid 1980s when comics began to pop up in the function rooms of London pubs. Gone were the old formulaic Irish and mother-in-law jokes replaced with rude, surreal and political ideas all sprinkled liberally with swearing. In those days the laughs were raw, and lack of polish was a virtue. You could shout and spit and if you happened to set fire to your genitals as well – all the better. It wasn't slick or honed but it was comedy back to its most elemental. No canned laughter. Not exactly difficult to organise either – a microphone and a light, and sometimes not even a light, or a microphone come to think of it. We queued round the block, then stood at the back and made one pint of cider last three hours. In those days they were alternative – alternative to the establishment. We used to know who that was then. These days everyone is alternative.

London 105 miles.

When we were growing up, comedians were working class fancy-dans, with bow ties and cummerbunds – and always with a boring song at the end. But the glitzy world of Saturday night telly always offered too much canned laughter for never enough joke. There'd be hours of crooning and energetic dance routines for just a few seconds of laugh out loud fun. Now I know why – guaranteed jokes are very expensive in both time and effort.

Uncle Eddie, now he was funny. Although Suzy and I seemed to be the only ones who could see it. Looking back, I think he was probably driven to creative rebellion under the shadow of his fearsome wife Maureen. He would tickle us, in the days when uncles were allowed to tickle children, and then sometimes he'd take out his false teeth and pull faces, usually when Auntie Maureen was going on a bit. He had jokes too, many of which I was disappointed to find on a souvenir Irish-joke tea towel a few years after he died. But he also had a rare gift for the non sequitur. He would often repeat a random word from a sentence giving it a whole new significance.

'We had a lovely time in Swanage this year' Auntie Maureen would declare.

'Swanage!' Uncle Eddie would shout for no reason, as if sure it was Nairobi.

'Mrs. Hopkins is in hospital again.'

'*Mrs?*' he would question, as if he was sure she was a mister. It didn't make sense but there was something about the conviction of his emphasis.

On other occasions he would take delight in making adults feel socially awkward. At one family gathering he produced a lit birthday cake and began to sing. As others joined in there was an air of tension as we approached the name and then . . . there was a gap. After a beat Uncle Eddie, Suzy and I fell about laughing – it was no one's birthday, but they'd all joined in like fools anyway.

I wasn't being racist was I? He was trying to break into my car, albeit by mistake. His colour was irrelevant. In fact it was only his colour that stopped me hitting him. Okay, his colour and his size.

Jonathan Wilkes. He was the first boy at school I noticed being sarcastic. He would reply to any obvious statement with a huge exaggerated 'NO!' and then put his tongue in front of his lower teeth to make the jaw of a Neanderthal. This was my first glimpse of rudimentary irony. 'Skill' was another one of his catch phrases. This followed anything that could conceivably bring him credit – getting a question right in class or having enough money to buy a packet of Refreshers.

I had to emulate him, and it wasn't long before I'd coached Suzy in the mystical ways of saying the opposite of what you meant, even if the timing took a little refining – I seem to remember causing a bit of a scene just after Granddad died and Grandma said tearfully 'He's gone and he's not coming back', and I chipped in 'NO! YOU DON'T SAY!'

According to my Mum, who met his mum recently, Wilkes is now running his own IT company in High Wycombe (Skill?).

79986 . . .

The first time Reg noticed a black man, when he was about three, he wandered up and pointed and said 'He's black!' I just stood there not knowing what to do. To be fair, the man just laughed.

I used to do a gag about the Islamic music festival being called Ramalamadingdong. But then one night an Asian woman cornered me after a show and insisted the joke was racist. Apparently 'ding dong, ding dong' is how other kids sometimes mimic Asian accents in the playground. News to me, but I dropped the gag. Not so much to stop Asian kids being bullied, but if I'm honest, more out of fear of being labelled racist.

Thinking to myself, I'm conscious of trying to please an invisible Lennie Parks beside me. The devil on my other shoulder is an imaginary Spaz Benson. He started out the same time as me, and we forged a friendship in the Bedlam of the open spot circuit. The freak show where you never quite know which ones are feigning madness. I didn't like him at first. He was a good-looking bloke who only seemed to have time for himself. But then we hit it off on a few car journeys and I found that beneath the smile and unreliability was a disarming honesty that was difficult not to like. These days he's the 'next big thing' and tipped to go far. He's a natural comic and when you're in his company sometimes you just have to stand back and become a grateful member of the audience.

79988 . . .

The first time I saw Spaz on stage, he broke all the rules. He admitted to being nervous, didn't get a laugh in the first 20 seconds, and then messed up a joke, an old one at that – and they still loved him. Now he's developed a style that appears entirely improvised, accepting and building on whatever's happening in the room. These days he seems to be able to rip the roof off any room at will, and can be very hard to follow. My writing feels leaden footed by comparison, as if I'm always destined to churn out Times New Roman in contrast to his Comic Sans. (Maybe it's because I'm a 'family man', which like a 'family car' and a 'family restaurant' means I'm generally popular, but seem to have a number of practical, but less than stylish built-in safety features.) Spaz also doesn't seem to care what he says either, which makes him all the more fascinating to watch. He would definitely have kept the Ramadan gag and probably added another about Mecca and bingo, only funny. Uninhibited charisma, that's what he's got, although sometimes, it seems to me, his fans seem to clap and cheer a little bit too much.

London 109.

Hang on! I'm getting further away! Turn round – go back through town. Here, in this drive. Who lives there? Perhaps I could knock on the door, introduce myself and start a new life here.

Now I'm stuck behind a tractor. Stuck behind a tractor at 1am, the wrong side of Norwich. I can never quite see enough road ahead to overtake before a bend. Move out to overtake. No, another bend. (Who drives a tractor in the middle of the night? An insomniac farmer, after eating his entire crop of carrots.)

Just passed a Little Chef. He seems to have done very well for himself – driven, no doubt, by hatred of his nemesis the Happy Eater.

Sometimes just telling the truth is the best policy. Big laughs can come out of stating the obvious. 'You're looking at me like you'd really like me to leave you alone', 'this bloke looks like he's about 12', 'That bit didn't go well'. It can really be that simple to get a big reaction. With a nervous audience, the laugh is often bigger than the joke.

In the same way addressing a large ethnic group or a party of disabled people, in an inclusive way, can be the right thing to do. Everyone knows they're there, all you're doing is relieving the tension. The only problem might be from those around them who feel that they should be offended on their behalf. I remember once I asked a man in the front row why he was sitting the wrong way round and he pulled out a white stick. The rest of the crowd fell silent. Then he bent his stick into a 'V' and waved it in my direction. The crowd cheered. The tension had gone. That's why Spaz is called Spaz. Years ago he took on a party of mentally disabled hecklers, and after the show they all wanted to hug him. No one else I know would have got away with it.

You can argue that if people watch comedy to see performers sail close to the wind, then they should chuck them a lifebelt when they capsize occasionally. Once I saw Tony Tundass taken to task by a Slovakian man for suggesting that he'd arrived in Britain underneath a lorry. Tony claimed he was being ironic. But then at the interval the asylum seeker produced a metal bar that was definitely more iron than ironic, and then Tony had to be smuggled out the building. Which really was ironic.

Kings Lynn. Queen's Derek.

There still aren't many women stand-ups. It's a solitary job after all, and there seem to be less women loners. Is it simply that women like talking to individuals and that men prefer to address groups? Maybe men are more threatened by a woman taking a lead. (Women sometimes seem quite threatened by women taking the lead too.) Well it's certainly harder for a woman to come up with a bulletproof persona, and most who succeed adopt the spiky approach.

It's lucky Marita's not vulnerable. Or is she? We're both working hard. The boys are a handful. I know I've set off early a couple of times just to get out of the house. Marita's still the main breadwinner. The cash I get covers extras. I'm the cake-winner. Must have an evening out together soon, just to catch up. But I know what will happen, we'll just both fall asleep.

Bury St Edmunds. Cremate Sister Sledge.

There's a dead badger by the side of the road. You'd notice if you hit a badger. Imagine being a badger living in Norwich. Perhaps it was suicide. And there's a flat rabbit too! Legs akimbo. None of them can stand it here. Cheap laughs though, making fun of Norwich. But you can't ban gags about stereotypes. That's what most jokes are, exaggerations of generalisations.

Where did the tractor go? I can't remember. The Ghost Tractor! Driven by the Ghost Farmer 'Oh Arrrrrh Oh Arrrrrrrrrrrh!'

It's all about the tone of what you say. Some acts – like Tony Tundass for instance – could make a Shakespeare sonnet sound like a dirty phone-call whereas someone else, with talent – Spaz – could probably make a dirty phone-call sound like a Shakespeare sonnet. But does getting a laugh make it right? Does anyone care? Although I suppose what someone laughs at shows where they're ticklish.

LONDON 100!
Oh come on, come on.

79999!

The best comics draw you into their own world. But the nuts and bolts of laughter aren't that funny. Recognition and surprise, that's what it's all about.

When comics watch a show they don't laugh with the audience. They laugh, not when the clown gets the custard pie in his face, but when the one he's expecting doesn't come. Their recognition comes from when it all goes wrong. Yes, if only the comics are laughing, you've either committed an act of genius or madness.

But sometimes I think I've forgotten how to laugh. Now I envy anyone who can roar out loud at the drop of a hat. I have to stand back, to know who's hat it is, why they dropped it, and then if I still think it's funny I'll just nod the nod of bored station guard inspecting a train ticket.

The car in front is weaving like a rally driver. I try and tuck in, and fly in his slipstream, but simply can't keep up. And as he heads towards another bend in the road I realise he's not even using his brakes. Just then a fluorescent arc of orange ash drops from the driver's window and disappears onto the road below. Smoking too! There's something hypnotic about watching someone with complete disregard for their own safety. Like some comics I know.

80002!

Prison IIII

This isn't funny. Five hours now. My fellow comics will surely do a benefit. Free the Manchurian One! There will be a rally in Trafalgar Square and a promoter will stand in front of a tank waving a good review of mine. Either that or they'll just divide up my material. (Mickey Spinola to the front of the queue.)

But will other comics stand up for me? Are they really my friends? How many times have I stood in the wings hoping the guy before me does well, but not that well? And how, when I've struggled, I've often willed the next act to do even worse so I don't look quite so bad? I'm not sure such jungle instincts make for loyalty.

Come on, it should be like the police – where 'officer down' means everyone swings into action to get justice for one of their own. Or will it be more a case of 'Officer down? – can I have his gigs please?'. (Somewhere there must be a policeman who's actually called 'Officer Down', who causes all sorts of confusion.)

Danny will do something. He'll drag Spaz in. Vince Matthews he'd definitely help out. Vince is black! One of my friends is black and I didn't even notice – that means I'm definitely not racist doesn't it? Perhaps I *should* have noticed. No I think I'm off the hook. I wish I was off the hook here.

When my boys find out I'm in prison will they tell everyone at school I'm a criminal? Will Marita be upset or will she just appreciate the break? Shouldn't there be a spider in here trying to spin a web or something who never gives up – and that teaches me a lesson about how to get through all this? I'd probably get the only spider who ever managed to hang himself in a web-making accident.

Suppose as a result of all this Britain goes to war with China? Then suppose a journalist unearths my old gag about being bullied at school and then rushed to hospital with 80 per cent Chinese burns? No, that's not going to help at all.

Tiredness Can Kill,
Take A Break

June 1995: Bristol to London by car

On a long drive it can be difficult to stay awake if you're on your own – you have to open the window, turn on the radio, or chew something. Normally it helps to have someone to talk to, but this time I'm giving a lift to Tony Tundass and he's rambling on and on about the clubs that won't book him. The window's open and I've been through two packs of wine gums, but I'm still fighting a losing battle with consciousness.

'. . . I wouldn't mind but it's not as if they offered us a drink.'

I've no idea what the first part of that sentence was. Leigh Delamere, Membury, Chieveley, Reading, Heston. These are the service stations on the M4 coming back from the West. Unlit until you reach Reading. The dials on the dashboard stare back at me like small black caves, or perhaps they're three mini covered stages at a tiny rock festival. Their numbers are approximate – my petrol gauge is about half full when it indicates 'a third', and if you travel for 60 miles at 60 miles an hour it always takes longer than an hour. There's a thin layer of dust on the matt black dashboard – you can't see it in the dark, but several times in the sunlight I've vowed to give it a wipe.

'That's the thing about bloody women comics isn't it?' he says flicking his hair back before re-tying the band holding his pony-tail.

'Yeah' mumbles the driver past caring what he's agreeing to.

Best keep inside these dotted lines, in case someone suddenly decides to cut along them with a giant pair of scissors. Sometimes, you can kid yourself that you are staying still; that it's the road that's moving, on rollers like a running machine.

'1986 wasn't it?'

'Er, something like that.'

We've just been to Bristol where I saved the show. Tundass was booed off after about seven minutes and I came on and did far longer than my 10-minute half spot, to fill the gap. It was a rough night, with lots of interrupting. But I'm learning how to deal with it now – to accept their ideas, and to run with their suggestions, boomeranging them back if I can. After all they've spent half an hour building up to their big moment, but they weren't banking on a conversation – you have a microphone, you should win.

Dealing with an unplanned interjection can look like magic. But people tend to shout out the same sorts of things – about how you look and what you say. After a while you're ready for them. But there are good and bad heckles, help and hindrance. Hindrance is negative, self indulgent, unclear. Help is positive, on subject, funny – but not too funny. (Although 'hindrance' poorly executed can turn into 'help'.) But the buzz of a new bit working – that's the best thing. When it's fresh, it's like gossip burning inside you, dying to be told.

Just then Tony laughs.

'Huh' I offer, ambiguously.

Bizarrely he thinks his gig was okay, but then Tundass is

notorious. He's been going for seven or eight years with limited success. He's what the listings describe as an 'experienced comedian'. Not 'funny', 'inventive' or 'stylish' or any of the other prefixes accorded to acts who've been around half the time he has. He still finishes with a card trick, which climaxes in him revealing the three of clubs tattooed on his chest (which at least shows commitment).

Behind his back the joke is that he's only booked by three clubs. His material is generic – you've seen something like it all before – he's really only doing an impression of a comedian, with routines about going to Amsterdam, cats and dogs and inbreeding in the West Country. (The last one being particularly ill advised this evening.)

'So do you think that would work?'
'Nah.'
'Why not?'
'What?! I don't know. Say it again.'
Drifted off there.

Occasionally there is a 'klunk', a line he persists with that doesn't work on any level but I fear these are just the ones he's written himself. In his hands good gags are wasted – like someone trying to shell pistachios with oven gloves.

In truth, his biggest problem is that on stage he's just not very likeable, or off stage, come to that. But crucially his skin is so thick he doesn't seem to care or notice, choosing instead to blame his lack of success on countless perceived vendettas. He's an unpredictable man and best given some space, like a car that's driving along with its indicator on for no apparent reason. He wants to know who's in with who, how much so and so pay and always, for some reason, how old people are.

'Forty nine!, Arnie Zoot is forty *nine*.'
He repeats with emphasis on the nine, which must mean he's in his forties too. Eventually Tundass begins to splutter less and less, like an engine that's getting used to dirty petrol, and now I

can just make out from the angle of my passenger's head that he's finally nodded off.

My back is soaked and I'm hunched over the steering wheel. Slowly I begin to relax. The moon is huge tonight, an enormous dusky pink. Perhaps it's a giant snooker ball skudding towards the earth, to pot us all into a black hole. Suddenly my passenger snorts in his sleep. Now I keep very still in case he starts up again, like one of those electric hand-driers that responds to movement.

'How much do the Bearpit pay in Durham? That cow won't return my calls . . .'

Too late.

But now I've had enough. Claustrophobic. Doesn't he get it? I've just had to clean up after him, like a dog-owner with a plastic bag. I was going to turn into these services coming up but if I put my foot down perhaps I can get it all over with a bit quicker.

'I'll tell you how you can bloody improve one of your gags . . .' he begins.

That's it!

'I'm just going to pull into these services and get a coffee.'

He carries on moaning while the car slows down, and as we get out, and stride across the car park towards the neon island. Here I'm delighted to meet Spaz and Pete Pendleton on their way back from Cardiff. It's quite common to meet other comics in the early hours. After all, on any one night there can be up to a hundred of us criss-crossing the country, tickling the regions. When we meet like this we talk like professional murderers comparing weapons and contracts.

'How were they?'

'I killed. There were these drunk guys on the left but I just kept hammering them.'

Individualists who can only be united for the briefest of causes – a journey or a coffee. On stage Pete is a cod French waiter. A character act with loud opinions, an eye for the ladies and 'would you like garlic breath with that?' When the crowd go with it he's difficult to follow – but when they don't, they really don't, and he has nowhere to go, apart from France I suppose.

It's apparently an ironic attack on British attitudes towards the French. But that's not always how some blokes in pubs see it. The longbow men of today are happy to settle for the perpetuation of a stereotype, unless the room I saw in Chelmsford chanting 'Kill the frogs!' were doing it in some sort of ironic way, of course. Off stage Pete behaves more like a shy accountant, and I know for a fact he enjoys bird watching. He'll end up on TV soon though, you'll see, he's an instinctive mimic and a good actor.

'Don't tell me, Tony's telling you all the clubs that won't book him' scorns Spaz.

'No no' I reply. 'We were talking about flower arranging.'

'Did you see that sign – Tundass can kill, take a break!' We all laugh, even Tundass, then incredibly, he starts up again.

'The Racoon in Cardiff won't book me either . . .'

'*That's because you're shit!*' Spaz explains thoughtfully.

(Good comics have a knack of getting to the point.) We all laugh, even Tony. Presumably he thinks it's a joke. Spaz has hit the nail on the head. But the nail hasn't noticed.

An elderly couple – the only others in the place – turn round. But, just as on stage, Spaz gets away with it because he does it with a smile. 'We're all monks on a day off' he explains.

The couple take it in good heart. Just then the extra chips Spaz has cajoled out of the girl behind the grill arrive. (Flirting in Berkshire at two in the morning.) I'd watched him do it. So naturally, so nicely – she melted from grungy teenager, embarrassed by her uniform, to giggling girl touching her tufty hair with long female fingers – a smiley Goth for goodness sake.

'How come you got chips?' says Tundass.

'Charm' says Spaz. 'You should try it sometime.'

'She fancies you doesn't she?' Spaz just shrugs.

'Why don't you introduce me if she comes back?' adds Tundass as if Spaz should have thought of it earlier.

'That'll make her night.'

Then Tundass begins to unwrap the cling-film from some sandwiches he's brought along, all this while droning on about more clubs and comics he has a grudge against.

'You know he won't offer you any petrol money either, don't you?' Spaz whispers to me.

Tightness: the coldest of vices. Just now Tony suddenly became preoccupied with the overhead menu when we all came to pay our bill at the checkout, hoping that someone would get his. The most frightening aspect of being addicted to scrimping is how it looks – that extra economy of self-awareness. I see Spaz has already hinted at some sort of rehab, by deliberately buying him two coffees.

Now everyone's laughing again. Spaz has got on to the tale of a magician we all know, who was employed by an old lady to do a show for what turned out to be her cat – well, it *was* his birthday. Tundass wants to know how much he got for it.

The smiley Goth is back. 'Excuse me sir, you're only supposed to consume food bought on the premises.'

Tundass finishes what's in his mouth. 'Really, your hair looks weird!'

There's a gap and then, all at once, the rest of us clutch or sides and spray into our sleeves in embarrassment. The girl retreats distinctly un-charmed.

We're in the Gents. 'Gentlemen' – the English often revert to an archaic language when dealing with anything that might cause embarrassment. A distancing over-politeness – a verbal pair of gloves – to help deal with an awkwardness of bodily function. Danny Bullen always calls me '*Mr* Stevens', and talks about 'repairing to a hostel for some beverages'. But I get on with him. I think I know what's happening behind his eyes and I trust his downbeat appraisal of people and situations. I don't understand Tundass.

Not all comics are depressed, but we all have a bit of grit that makes us who we are. Sometimes I think Spaz is trying to escape from some terrible secret. (But I can't help thinking of the prisoner who escaped from Colditz by feigning madness, but when he arrived back in England he had to be admitted to an asylum.)

Growing up, most of us were outsiders: geeks, bullied, bullies, service kids. Constantly finding ways to fit in or to stand out, whatever would make us accepted. It's just now we've turned professional. Marita says I'm passive aggressive. At first I didn't think anything of this – then I got really angry, well that's what would have happened in a sitcom. But it's not like other jobs. You can start off bad, get good, and then go bad again. (About how many comics do people say 'I preferred their early stuff'?)

But Danny's act has been the same for years – a time capsule from the early nineties replete with references to *Trainspotting* and John Major. He makes a living by sheer unpretentious persistence. Having a thick skin of course can also make you insensitive, and Tundass is fast becoming a walking cautionary tale. Am I like him and no one will tell me?

We drift back to our cars, but Tundass lingers in the Gents, after all he did finish both the coffees that were bought for him. Spaz dares me to drive off without my passenger. I accept his suggestion, get into the car and drive off, laughing all the way until just before Reading. From here on, the motorway is lit, and now it doesn't seem quite so funny. Briefly I consider going back to get him. Briefly.

Prison ЦѰ

It's a drug. Nothing is more important than the next funny. Even when not working, I'm always trying to think what gags I could use if unexpectedly called upon – at a bus stop, a supermarket checkout, or even at a funeral. I rarely get to do them, of course, but I just can't seem to help myself from being ready if necessary. The other week I asked in front of a crowded garage waiting room, if they'd got any special offers like 'Four new tyres for the price of one!'. Got a good laugh from a van driver sitting next to me.

Sitting here in the stinking cold I'm still trying to think of what I should have said from the back of the lorry, to everyone gathered in the street just before I was taken away.

Oh yes, there was that time an AA man was trying to recruit members outside the supermarket – I asked him to take a look at my trolley's wonky wheel. That didn't even have an audience – that was just for me! He certainly didn't laugh.

Always beachcombing, living between two worlds, seeing what the tide brings in and then trying to make something out of it. Dancing as the waves chase me up the sand. They say we all emerged from the ocean after all. That's probably why old people retire to the seaside.

It's cold turkey in here though. There's nothing remotely amusing about this place. It just doesn't seem very fair that's all. Sure I've done a few things I'm not too proud of, but nothing, nothing really. I'm a good guy. This is all a big misunderstanding. Yes I'm even getting a little bit cross now. Steady.

Beware! Thieves Operate In This Area

October 1995: Car from
Folkestone to London

Now I'm heading back to London. My foot is on the floor, I'm doing 85 and I'm furious. This is difficult to swallow, like a big fat greasy oven chip.

'Plagiarism!' someone shouts at me halfway through a student gig.

'Four syllables, that's good for Folkestone University' I reply. Then it dawns on me what they've said. So I check.

'What did you say?!'

'Mickey Spinola used that line on TV last night.'

'Oh' I reply. (It's my line, Spinola's the plagiarist.) Then I ask the runt his name, what he's studying. No reply. 'What, you find that out in your second year do you?'

Laughter and jeers, then we get on with the show.

Afterwards, Sid the ents. manager is smiling. (Like most ents. managers he looks like a pirate – black T-shirt, earrings and a pony-tail – although unsurprisingly he's failed to organise a parrot.) 'I thought that's where you'd got it!' he beams.

I give him a withering look. Why would I knowingly nick the joke of someone famous that they'd used on TV last night?

Student gigs are as good as the enthusiasm of the person running it. This one started late, no one knew how to turn off the fruit machines at the back of the room, and during the interval someone nicked the microphone. I ended up standing on a table shouting at people.

At the interval I call home, and sure enough Pete Pendleton has phoned to say he saw Spinola do my stuff on the box last night.

A brand new VW Polo (smug) shoots past, and as it pulls in front, sends windscreen washer fluid up into the air like a stubby little whale showing off.

Mickey Spinola was a young mainstream act when alternative comedy broke out. He adapted by charming audiences and brazenly borrowing the material of the less famous. Apparently, if ever confronted, he blames his writers. Sure enough, it's them who go round and cream off the best from the rest, but he's been warned too many times now, not to know what they do.

The truth is, he doesn't care. He conveniently observes the old tradition of if it's 'out there' then anyone can use it. Well his car is 'out there' somewhere too, I wonder how he would feel if I nicked that? That wouldn't be such a bad idea – get the Press involved. Although, thinking about it, his car is probably made from bits of other people's cars.

Wouldn't happen in any other art form. Oh no, not in music, fine art, literature – they would all go to court. But which up and coming comic wants to be known for suing someone, rather than for being funny?

Must put my seat belt on. (Except now I'm not sure if it's riskier to put it on while moving.) And now it's beginning to rain: just enough for the windscreen wipers to smear the window and then groan with dryness. Out of windscreen wash too – Spinola's probably siphoned it off.

Sure, when comics start out their style often appears a bit like someone else's, but if they're any good they soon develop a voice of their own. In the old days (pre-1980s) it was common practice for comedians to 'share' material, because often a lot of their patter was a mixture of old pub gags and folklore. They could get away with this because performances were live and mostly to just a few hundred people at a time. But once a joke has been on telly you can't use it ever again. Okay you can, but not for a while.

It's raining properly now. I feel like King Lear in the storm. King Lear in a car in the storm. Cursing fate and the elements with all my rage, but with a tiny Magic Tree air freshener hanging from the mirror.

Sure there are grey areas – heckle put downs and certain MC-ing techniques that a lot of people seem to use – but I guess exceptions are made because of it being a potentially make or break situation. But this is just theft, and I feel assaulted. Except it's not just theft, it's replication, and most audiences will assume that what they see on TV is the original and what they hear in the backroom of a pub is the copy.

A stick man in a little red pyramid – is he digging a pile of triangular dirt or trying to pick up a Christmas tree? Road works ahead! The final insult: injustice, rain and gridlock, and it's 1.30 in the morning. Eight hundred yards – then three lanes down to two. Most of us are already queuing in two lanes, but the occasional chancer shoots down the outside to cut in at the front of the line. That's the way it is now. Stand-up will soon be a course at university, you'll see – everyone is desperate to have a go. Look at them jumping the queue and going straight to telly. I won't be letting anyone cut in tonight.

Sometimes routines are lifted from across the Atlantic, or whole acts can turn up translated into Swedish or Afrikaans. But individual joke theft is difficult to prove, after all, everyone deals in them. They're exchanged at school, at work and in pubs. People just want to laugh, they don't care where the gag comes from. It hurts more than I thought it would – like someone passing off your child as their own.

Of course, it's possible to think of the same joke as someone else, after all there are only so many subjects and so many formulas. It's also true that in the heat of the moment you might come up with certain words a little too easily and only realise later that they belong to someone else. But amongst ourselves we know who the magpies are, the junkies who have to keep robbing to support their habit.

Anger usually takes a little while to trickle through my system, but this has me clench-jawed and white-knuckled already. I've a good mind to drive up to the West End and see if I can find him. Don't know why I think he's there, but at this moment it seems worth taking the chance. I mean I've had concepts nicked before. Gags driven into the workshop, serial numbers removed, then re-sprayed and driven out as new. But Spinola doesn't even try. He nicks jokes and then uses them even in the same order as his victim did.

Two lorries are overtaking each other and blocking the whole road. When I get up close there is a huge blinding spray from both of them, I'm going to have to take them both on the outside. But the gap's a bit too small. My sphincter tightens.

'Come on, come on.'

I use my horn. Not that they can hear it, or could even go any faster if they wanted to. It's a Dutch lorry overtaking a Polish one. Off the ferry, probably – full of clogs and potatoes respectively. Alien typefaces. But they both know the inter-national language of juggernauts. A dip of the headlights to say it's safe to pull in front, then, when the manoeuvre is complete, a flick of the hazard lights by the new leader of the convoy. It's all nods and winks amongst professionals. I wonder if the same move is repeated in the café at the Services when Johan, who is ready to pay, has to overtake Lech who is still waiting for his soup?

I can always write another joke. But then he can always steal it again. It's the principle. If I had unlimited money I'd hire a private detective to search through all old scripts and tapes to see who's nicked what. Then I'd burst into their workshops in the middle of the night – sending tools and spray paint flying and get them to sign a confession . . . which wouldn't work . . . cos none of them can write, of course . . . . I AM SO ANGRY!

I swish down the M40 slicing through the folds of rain; the wipers have to work harder now to clear my vision.

Part of me doesn't want to confront Spinola at all. I might have pity on him. He probably has a son in a wheelchair, or something. Well, he will have when I've finished.

'I suppose it's a compliment, him stealing your joke' said the ents. manager.

A pirate would say that.

Prison ✝ I

Voices. The door scrapes open. A guard mumbles something. I notice his uniform doesn't really fit properly. Then he motions for me to get up. At the door he's joined by another bigger soldier, whose uniform fits better. Neither of them speaks. I'm still shaking with cold. Except it's not cold. It's fear! I haven't shaken with fear for 30 years – a playground fight, being sent to the headmaster. This could be a combination of both. (That's not counting before and during all open spots, of course.)

The middle-aged officer is sitting behind a desk, smoking. Apparently Good Cop couldn't make it today. He looks a bit like a Chinese version of a neighbour I know in Ealing. A neighbour whose cat craps on our lawn. (Since I've been here I've seen several Asian versions of people I know back home. Is that racist? And I wonder if it works the other way round?)

With the disdain of a professional bully Chairman Miaow gestures for me to step forward. He says something in Chinese. I'm sure I heard him speak English before, and he can be pretty sure I can't speak his language. Then he shouts the same thing again in my face. His breath – what is it like? Yes, like rancid air from a bicycle inner tube. The two guards laugh in a slightly forced way. It's a bit like a film. So this is what it's like to be an ethnic minority who's the butt of a joke.

By this time I've got control of my fear and my instinct is to fight back. (After all I've spent years training to win arguments.) At that moment the best I can manage is to make something up that sounds like Chinese, and I shout it at them. Then I repeat it, but this time, to my horror I put my fingers into the corners of my eyes and pull the skin tight in a 'slanty little eyes' fashion. Bad move. Where did *that* come from? That wouldn't be in a film. What was I thinking?

They all stare at me for what feels like about four days. This has changed things. *Where* did that come from? My reaction was completely disproportionate. Someone's dropped a shuttlecock gently over the net and I've walked round and smashed my racquet down over their head. Chairman Miaow's picked up on my insolence and probably the implied racism too. Now all I can think of is to say 'I've had Chinese people up to here' (holding hand three feet off the ground). But I don't. The officer rips up a piece of paper and issues an order. What was that, 'Take him away'? 'Shoot him at dawn?' 'Feed him to the dragon?'

'Listen this is all a big mistake . . . .' I say, the words trailing off as I realise I've just taken the screenplay back into cliché.

Alone in the cell again. Before, I felt I definitely didn't deserve this, now I'm not so sure. No! I could have handled that better, but I still shouldn't be here. I'm wrongly accused – don't even know what of yet. Perhaps I would have found out if I hadn't . . . . I can't believe I did that thing with the eyes.

Now I really, really want to go home. Badly.

Delays Until August 1996

Direct from Edinburgh to Broadway, Ealing Broadway – three more stops and I'll be back home. Can't wait to see them all again. Three more stops in my stop-start career. Away almost a month, living as a bachelor; Marita has kept the boys in London. The grass is brown; it must have been warmer down here than it was up there, not that I've seen much daylight in the last four weeks. This is what it must feel like coming home after the war.

I feel battle hardened now. I've been in the trenches with the lads, looked the enemy in the eye and even got a taste for killing. I've been promoted too. You have to be promoted if you want to be part of the Edinburgh Festival. Promoters arrange the show. But now I have some momentum – know what I'm about and other people are even beginning to know who I am, too.

These days the Edinburgh Fringe has been taken over by comedy. There are hundreds of shows and most involve some kind of stand-up. There are various competitions of course to help create a buzz – best in breed, largest innuendo, that sort of thing. Normally I have disdain for contests that try to compare chalk with cheese. I mean, if the chalk is really chalky and the cheese is really cheesy, who's to say – it's all subjective, surely.

But now I'm not so sure. For once, this year doesn't seem quite so much about the Emperor's brand new summer collection – I wonder where I should keep my award? Yes, I won one, did I not mention that? Suddenly the Fringe seems like a place where the top comedy fashion houses set the trends before they filter down to the off the peg routines on the High Street. Winning awards is the upside of showbiz. Plumbers don't win awards.

An endless panorama of the backs of houses. Some gardens are full of plastic toys left where they were dropped. Others are a monument to neglect and a half-hearted trip to a garden centre. Have they forgotten that they have an audience pass by once every 10 minutes! I just think I'd try a bit harder. Sell the lawn as advertising space, put up a sign saying 'The brakes have gone, throw us your valuables!' or perhaps, dress up as Isambard Kingdom Brunel or Queen Victoria and leap up and down on a trampoline when the trains go past. Yes, a different famous person from history every day.

The Scottish capital is a city on a hill under siege. Many of the buildings balance on the edge of spectacular drops, their gothic facades looking down with dour disdain on the frivolity beneath.

But no one under 30 wants to visit the castle, it's all about the theatres, halls and cowsheds jammed full to see the clowns. Secretly I've always wondered how much of what is fan-fared at the Fringe would actually work in front of a real audience. My aunt and uncle in Crewe for instance. In fact Uncle Larry might square up to a comic or two as he has an aversion to any kind of swearing where ladies are present. But I think that they're more of a normal audience than your average Fringe punter . . . who's called Russ, studies Media at Salford and wears silly designer glasses.

If you're involved in a show at the Fringe it feels like the whole world is watching – and I suppose most of mine is – there are reviews in the big dailies and all sorts of radio and TV shows that come 'live' from the army of temporary venues that are all camped round the castle. But it's the summer, and the rest of Britain is on holiday so ultimately it's of far less significance than it feels at the time. But it's also a menagerie of sights and sounds you'll never hear anywhere else in the world, ever. This year I shared a dressing room with an Australian transvestite who does immaculate Shirley Bassey impressions and a teenage choir from Soweto.

Down south, a whole month of blue skies and ice creams has gone by without me.

This year I'm determined not to read any reviews, but walking past my venue one lunchtime, the girl on the door holds up a copy of the *Scotsman* and shouts 'Look what they've done to you!' Feigning casualness I saunter over and pick up the paper, then my stomach turns as I scan the copy. It's a nasty shock like suddenly being mentioned in a school assembly. 'Poor', 'self indulgent' and 'over-long' are the words I pick out immediately. There are a few balancing compliments but they're of little consolation. It's by someone called David Ingham and I'm already mentally constructing his epitaph – 'out of touch', 'wrong' and 'sudden death' are the words you might pick out.

All the critics I've ever met have offered the guilty handshake of a traffic warden who doesn't own a car; a referee who knows they can never be a player. No matter how well written their review, they still can't make a room full of people laugh for an hour. So what do they know?

Although, obviously if you get a good review that's different. Obviously that would be from an expert who knows what they're talking about, a veritable connoisseur of talent with an ear to the ground and a nose for the zeitgeist. (Although hopefully they don't use the word 'zeitgeist'.)

Doesn't everyone have a lot of cars down here? They're like extra rooms I suppose – mobile conservatories. I haven't driven for a month.

Previously I've been to the Fringe on bills of three or four, but this is my first one-man show. An hour is a long time to make people laugh for. An average audience's concentration is about 40 minutes without a break. You have to pace yourself, then perk things up somehow with music or sound effects. The challenge is to make every member of the audience feel like they're the only person in the room. Of course, if your show's not doing well, they might well *be* the only person in the room. Some days, for my show, there were no tickets sold at all, they had to give them away.

Night after night all the same people in the same bars. The hills, the beer, the cobbles and the queues – permanently excited and bored at the same time, and always with the sound of bagpipes in the background. A desperate annual circus, like that crazy day in summer when all the flying ants emerge.

Several others are in contact during the day, saying that Ingham has 'got it wrong', that he's 'out of order'. Eric Bowman says Ingham only writes good reviews for Telestar acts.

Also while up in the mist, I play Spaz at badminton. He's looking a little more middle aged having put on some weight since I saw him last, as if someone's slightly inflated him with a bicycle pump. We find a court free in the University and it's good to get rid of some aggression and begin to ease the build-up of adrenaline and alcohol. Given that he hasn't played much before he's pretty good. He hits the shuttle naturally – I should have known he would. With a bit of practice he would probably be better than me.

'You thrashed me Stevens' he groans lying flat on his back.

But it feels like I've lost. There's something about him that makes you want him to succeed. Sure enough, then he waves to two girls who've been watching from the gallery. Giggling, they wave back saluting the loser.

Great. Last night I watched him brush off a third admirer with consummate but brutal charm.

'You must get a lot of female attention' she says giving him her best vulnerable stare. 'How *do* you handle it all?'

'Oh you, know' he shrugs puffing smoke to one side.

Then she leans forward to solicit a light, cigarette still in mouth. She receives the ember like a Chinese Whisper, pulls back and then releases smoke sideways.

Spaz continues. 'Yuh I usually talk to them for a bit, then make some kind of ridiculous excuse.'

He smiles. She smiles back. Then she tilts her head in case this new angle somehow increases her attractiveness.

'And does that work?' she pouts.

'Oh yeah' he says 'Always.' He puffs again and sends his smoke skywards like a steam train.

Then he looks at his watch. 'Listen, I'm going to have to go, my aunt has got mumps and I'm looking after her parrot.'

They both laugh. Then he leaves and doesn't come back. It takes her a while to realise, then I have to look away.

Resting on the jolly plaid of the train seat, suddenly I'm overcome with tiredness. The afternoon sun seems very bright and all I want to do is curl up and fall into a bottomless hole. Tonight will be the first time I haven't performed in four weeks.

David Ingham is pointed out to me across the courtyard. He's wearing one of those Tibetan hats, and he can't be more than 25. A short life. I imagine telling the police how I strangled him.

'His death was . . . poor . . . overly long too.'

No, I'll bide my time. Don't let him see you watching him, don't let him know that you care. I'm on to you Ingham.

Just outside the station the train stops and waits for a platform to become available. The engine revs. This is tortuous. The train lurches forward again and I go and stand at the door.

The next review is a good one – can't remember who wrote it. But whether they like you or not, they always quote your best lines, and not always correctly. Also, quoted verbatim, the black and white drains the words of tone and context, and the reader's eye is able to race to the end and guess any surprise. This must be how Shakespeare feels, looking down as an English teacher points out a 'joke' in the text, to incredulous teenage pupils.

Our road has fewer cars in it than I remember – most people are still away. A breeze does a Mexican wave through the trees and up above an emerald Aer Lingus 737 makes a beeline for Terminal One. Perhaps it's more like being let out of prison than coming home from the war. At least Marita hasn't received a telegram saying that I'd died in action. ('Acton', more likely.)

There are all sorts of awards of course – best live performance, best character-act, best musical act. The sort of hairsplitting differences you deride until you win one. But if you were about to land an award you'd think the organisers would make sure you were going to be there. I received no such tip off and went along as an after-thought, out of curiosity and boredom. Last year's winner opened the envelope. My first thought was that this year's winner had the same name as me! Then it was up on to the stage – quick before they change their minds. I grab the Champagne and thank a long list of people, leaving some out, of course.

In truth it's a very pleasant surprise, in fact there's even a hint of embarrassment that it suddenly means so much. Perhaps I'm keener to 'play the game' than I thought. So after several long years of two steps forward, one point eight seven steps back, I'm the 1996 Schweppes Best Newcomer. All my dogged commitment has paid off. Just as well really, I was on the verge of giving up.

What will the kids make of it I wonder? Perhaps I'll tell them it's like getting a gold star for doing your homework. Fortunately it *is* a big gold star. At the time I was stunned. Only now, a few days later am I properly elated. Relieved too. Relieved and feeling justified, I suppose. We might even all join hands and jump up and down on the bed. That's what we did when Stan was, at last, potty-trained.

I've missed the little rascals. Even the nightly riot of screaming, splashing and flying chicken nuggets. When I phoned last week Marita told me of how she'd caught them both throwing flowers over the fence in the garden. Under cross examination Reg explained how they'd accidentally thrown a Frisbee over, and now they were chucking the flowers over too so the neighbour would smell them, come out into the garden and throw the Frisbee back. It was brilliant: either logic, or improvisation.

Well at least I have something to show for my missing summer. Also now it seems that writing a joke is not as hard as it used to be. Doing a set is like filling the dishwasher. Packing it in so there are no gaps, but still making sure everything gets what it deserves.

That's right, I don't rehearse what I'm going to say anymore, I just get up and do it. Instinctively too, I now ask a question to the crowd once in a while to vary the dynamic. Improvising is the most exciting, stepping off the path, doing a little dance in the jungle and then running back to the well-blazed trail without getting lost. A lot of gigs in a short time have made me sharp, like an athlete who knows what he's good at; confident, or perhaps just tired of being nervous. No longer do I need to take all gigs everywhere for any kind of money, I can pick and choose. Well, a bit.

Passing the betting shop I notice the photos are about 10 years out of date. Famous golfers when they had hair, footballers long since retired. I'm already halfway to a line about a Time machine sponsored by Ladbrokes when I remember that if you talk about sport you lose half the room. No, not enough people will have noticed this.

Playing with words and ideas all the time. Using adrenaline to focus thoughts so that they emerge already edited. Because getting it wrong in front of a crowd is like being hit with a great big stick, and after a while you begin to anticipate its trajectory.

Up the path. The grass needs cutting. The house is quiet. We all say hello again. Well what was I expecting – bunting? Reg and Stan are tanned and have noticeably grown. They take me and my award in their stride. It's strangely quiet. Marita suggests they play outside in the sandpit with the plastic dinosaurs I've brought them from Scotland. I'm back in the land of toys – paradoxically this means I have to start acting like a grown up again. The barbecue has already been covered and packed away for the winter, although it reminds me of something . . .

Being alone with Marita snaps me out of this daze. She's never looked finer. That's the thing about coming home after a while away, like returning to a joke you're trying to write – for a few seconds you can see things objectively, before the grey mist of familiarity descends again. I'm a lucky man.

But something's wrong. Marita's not her usual self. I sense a 'chat' coming and I have to break the spell.

'What!?' I say, finally.

'Suzy has cancer.'

But it doesn't register. Ah, that's right the hooded barbecue looks like it's being held hostage by the tipped up garden chairs surrounding it.

'Did you hear what I said?'

'Er yup, cancer.'

Request Stop

September 1996: Bus from London to home

There's a chill in the air. That bloke never used to speak to me. But everybody wants to know me since Edinburgh. I won't be travelling on buses like these much longer. I'll have my own bus. Like a rock band, with security, groupies and a manager, maybe.

Gary Bidulph has phoned from Telestar Management. He says he's always liked my stuff and would love a meeting. We meet at a little place he knows – a Lebanese coffee shop in Soho. (Arnie Zoot signed with them a month ago and they filled up his diary straight away!) We sit at a table outside catching the last of the autumn sun. I wear jeans and a jacket with sunglasses perched on my head. At the last minute I'd managed to remove a bright white earring – a marooned dab of shaving foam.

Bus seat-cover material is like no other. It's like sitting on Christmas jumpers all year round.

Agents are like buses ... aren't they? They must be somehow .... Let's see, even when you get one you can't help wondering whether another one would've been better? No, you've got a funny feeling that in the end you're going to have to change, to get where you want to go. Or perhaps in the end it would have been quicker to walk on your own.

'*How are you?*' he exclaims managing to put emphasis on all three words.

'Yeah, good' I reply, using the 'yeah' to parry his enthusiasm. But I'm not good; the potential shadow over Suzy is at last beginning to darken my outlook. I don't want to get too cozy, so I order a cool mineral water.

'Still or sparkling?' says the waiter.

'Fizzy' I say – the word 'fizzy' suddenly sounding disappointingly childish.

I've known Bidulph since he used to collect the money on the door of the Roaring Monkey in Streatham. Since then he's gone on to work for the big boys. I should be flattered. But in the light of other events even my award means almost nothing. Almost.

'You look tired mate, you haven't caught up since Edinburgh have you?'

'Nah.'

Agents have thick skins but they can sniff out weakness over huge distances, like a raptor in *Jurassic Park*.

These single-deckers make it impossible to thank the driver as you leave by the door in the middle. You have to hang about at the bus station and then follow them home.

The agents and promoters I've had to deal with so far have been a little further down the food chain – nocturnal beings surviving off scraps and droppings in the shadows, blagging a living off the goodwill of venues and naïve ambition of performers. They're not all bad, but those at the bottom of the greasy pole seem to be the greasiest.

Telestar have a TV production company. They look after a lot of big names. They also have the reputation of being arrogant bullyboys, holding small clubs to ransom for huge fees, threatening to withdraw their big names if their newer acts don't get on the bill as well. But we all need a buffer. A shock absorber to help us cope with being a commodity, or a scapegoat to blame when we want to play it tough.

I'm actually planning to go with Gordon Heath a middle range agent who seems as genuine as an agent can be. Besides I don't want to work for organised crime. But it can't hurt to just hear what they say can it?

Cancer! It's not fair. She's just had a baby. Zoe will want for nothing. Except a mother, possibly.

Gary is nicer than I remember, and he makes a point of laughing at all my jokes. Even the ones I don't mean. Funny bones, that's what I've got. Perhaps I should go with Telestar.

'In a few years you could be the new Patrick Fredericks!' he says.

He's obviously very knowledgeable about the business. (Who's Patrick Fredericks?)

He also loves what I do with my 'panda material'. He says it's a simple routine with layers of irony.

Lots of people survive it these days. Name one.

He says I'd have to sign up for five years. And they would get 15 per cent of everything, but they would see it as an investment. Nice of them. I'll go with Gordon.

Ralph's Mum. She had an operation a few years ago. She's in remission. That's what they call it. And if they can't cure it? Remission Impossible.

Gary wants to know if I'm interested. My recent success has given me a bit of confidence. I pause, lift my drink to prolong the moment, but the coaster sticks to the bottom of the glass and I put it down sharpish.

'I'm going to think about it.'

'Very wise' he replies. (Although I get the feeling if I'd decided to go with them on the spot that would have been 'very wise' as well.)

Just as my new friend Gary leaves, he adds 'Well, my people will be in touch with your people.'

I smile. But I haven't got any people; I thought that was the point of our meeting? Now all I can think of is our respective teddies and Action Men meeting up for a picnic. I'm definitely going with Gordon.

She's started radiation treatment already. Mum and Dad will be beside themselves. I've been thinking about her a lot recently. About Bexhill, growing up and our unspoken bond. Not so much peas in a pod, as a carrot and a potato stewed in the same juice.

He's got to catch a plane. I thank him for seeing me. But thinking about it, *he* asked to see *me*. Like all successful bullies he makes you want to please him, even thank him for bullying you. He says a friendly goodbye to the Arab patron. (Telestar probably represent the PLO.)

He leans forward. 'You sure you're alright mate?'

'I can't find my sunglasses' I mumble for something to say.

He laughs. 'They're on your head mate!'

For some reason this slip becomes an emotional trigger, and just then I begin to choke up. Wrong time, wrong place. Gary doesn't seem to notice, or does he? Perhaps he just blanks it, he probably won't have the emotional software for dealing with it anyway. He just prattles on about needing to get to the airport but then he looks at me.

'Are you sure you're okay?'

'Yeah fine.'

Then I raise my glass to my lips for something to do, making sure I hold the coaster down this time. But there's nothing left to drink and the ice and lemon just slide down against my nose. Placing the glass back on the table I have to say something.

'Just hungry really.'

'Order some food mate. Anwar! Mr. Stevens wants a sandwich!'

'What? Oh right. No I'm . . . .'

Telestar are becoming big players in the media. Perhaps I should go with them. They're a public company now and investing in new technology and foreign networks. No, I think I'm better off with a smaller agent. Someone small and hungry. Like the Happy Eater. Gordon it is.

Gary pauses at the curb. 'Your own TV show within three years, that would be my plan.'

Them! Them! Them!

Then he bundles into a taxi, which seems to have been waiting for him. There's some mineral water left in the bottle he ordered – about 15 per cent. There's a joke there, but I don't quite have the will to put it together. I reach for my sunglasses. But they're not on my head anymore; it just feels like they are. I've put them in my pocket. Sunglasses in October – who do I think I am?

I go and wait for a bus. The bus comes, I get on, and then I get off at the next stop, cross the road and wait on the *correct* side of the road. Perhaps I'm not quite myself at the moment. But it's difficult to tell; I'm always doing things like that.

Prison ЖН II

Not long after that of course, Bidulph took on Mickey Spinola. They formed an ugly combination – naked ambition and bare cheek. Slowly, Spinola's star began to rise and rise, Bidulph on the ground below, pointing at the sky until he'd attracted a crowd. TV slots, presenting, everywhere you turned – 'this week's special guest Mickey Spinola', 'coming soon Mickey Spinola's much awaited first TV series', 'the news was read by . . .' etc.

Still here, still shaking. I have a pretty good internal clock – well I know what an hour feels like. This has been at least the length of quite a few one-man shows. At first I felt a sort of righteous indignation at being here, but since the 'racial incident' I feel more than a twinge of guilt, shame even. Most galling of all is the thought that they might have been going to release me until I did what I did. It's not as if I can even explain or apologise.

Where did it come from? Stress? I wouldn't have done that on stage. If I had, I would have had bouncers to protect me. But here the whole audience are bouncers, bouncers with guns, and I've just personally insulted all of them. Let's hope they see the funny side. Is there one? Come on – I feel like I'm coming apart at the seams already, like an inadequate bin liner stuffed with coat hangers.

A good bouncer is hard to find. It's a mistake to dismiss them all as neck-less meatheads. A good doorman smiles occasionally, diffuses trouble before it gets out of hand. They go in, have a word, draw a line in the sand, and if it still kicks off, it's all over very quickly. 'Bad bouncer' makes a scene, thinks he's Chuck Norris. His ear-piece is for the management to remind him how to walk in a straight line 'Left right, left right'. 'Good bouncer' offers the persistent heckler a joke explaining service – outside now. Usually doormen aren't bad judges of comics either. They see a lot of acts; know who's got a glass chin, and who knows how to work the ring. But these prison guards aren't bouncers – they're just kids. Conscripts. They may not have seen a Westerner up close before. They don't seem that interested either.

I wonder when my family will find out, or whether they know already.

There don't seem to be any sounds from other prisoners. Perhaps they're all dead. Will I survive? Imagine if Gloria Gaynor was in the cell next door. I'd ask her if she thinks that she's going to get out of here. And then she'd look at me, and I'd look at her, and she'd say 'No'.

What if my outburst was caught on CCTV? The tapes might end up back home. 'COMIC IN NAZI OUTBURST SHOCKER!' says the *Sun*. The *Daily Mail* will run a campaign to get me released; the *Guardian*, one to get me shot.

From this distance showbiz is beginning to seem like a crappy little Wendy house, and I feel like a fool for trying so hard to get in the door. There are nearly a billion and a half Chinese, and none of them know who I am! Think about something else.

I spy, with my slanty little . . .

For Hire

November 1996: Taxi back from
TV company

What is that noise these taxis make? Like a mechanical panting dog.

I didn't want to get a cab, but the production company has called me one, and I don't want to lose face. I prefer to lose 35 quid instead. I doubt this cabbie will accept my Travelcard. Now we're stuck in Camden High Street edging along at about 50 pence a metre. It's busy, very busy – they should extend the congestion charge as far as . . . Belgium. Paris? No, Belgium. Sillier word – a mixture of belly and gum. Bilge and tum.

As always it's fancy dress day round here. Dodgy people wearing dodgy clothes and selling dodgy stuff. We're even stopped long enough for a Rasta, wearing the sort of hat that would make even Dr Seuss cringe, come up to the open window and say, dodgily, 'Hash?'

'Yes indeed, that's what you're making of your life!' I would have said if the incident was on stage, unlikely though that would be. Although, it's amazing what gets produced these days.

Barry Whitlow is a top TV executive at Rushwood Studios. He has an engaging Dublin brogue, which should mean he's from Ireland, although I wouldn't be surprised if he picked it up on a course he went on to make him sound more friendly.

On the phone he's conspiratorial, always with a compliment to offer, like a winning uncle with a bag of sweets. Take your pick – 'It's a crime you're not on television', 'You're the best in the country at what you do' and 'I'm really excited about our meeting'. I should have listened to my instinct as well as the clicking of his keyboard, just audible under his sweet nothings, as he wrote to someone else at the same time as talking to me – his answers coming slightly delayed as if he was on some sort of satellite link-up. I'm guessing he's not 'excited' about our meeting at all, at best he's mildly intrigued. If he was that excited he wouldn't have cancelled it twice already.

Well, it's his constant slating of others that gives him away, others to whom you've seen him offer the same compliments. I guess I'm just a pie he wants to stick a finger in. In case I'm the next big pie, and then he'll have a slice of me.

His PA, Farah, who has blonde flicky hair and a bare midriff, shows me past corridors full of photos of previous Rushwood successes. *The Wilf Cartwright Show*, *Mansfield or Bust*, the cast of *Pop and the Weasel*. She's full of sunny chitchat; although I notice her default setting word is 'cool'. In the same way Eskimos are supposed to have nine words for snow, Farah seems to have one word for nine different things. ('Snow's probably one of them.') Her crop-top and exposed belly remind me of a pencil case with a sliding lid, that you can just push along to see what's inside.

My new agent, Gordon (in the cold light of day I opted for a private investigator rather than a terrorist) has put me in touch with Barry. When we meet, his eyes are bright and expectant, as if he's permanently 'just discovered treasure'. We shake hands and sit down in what is the mini-living room part of his office – a couple of leather sofas in front of a coffee table where all the daily papers are laid out beside a few empty wine bottles.

'Sorry, would you mind getting rid of those Farah, we had a few drinks last night with Penny Bennett! We've just got a second series!'

'Excellent' I say, hating myself as I do it, because I really loathe that show. But there's something about Barry's intensity and his 'like me' eyebrows that makes me want to please him.

'Sure' says Farah, with the flicky hair, gathering the bottles and then we both try not to watch her wiggle out the door. Then Barry leans forward with a lopsided grin. Last time I saw him was in a bar in Edinburgh when he was off his head on coke, his eyeballs and jaw wriggling about as if to try to escape the skin they were trapped in.

'So what are you up to mate?'

Over to me – now is the time to sparkle. So I try and make 'not much' sound as much as possible, recounting the tale of a Christmas gig where Roy Bracewell got pelted off with mince pies.

'That's funny!' says Barry – as if he'd recently been appointed as the Supreme Judge of what's funny and what's not. 'Oh Spaz Benson sends his love by the way, I saw him yesterday about something.'

'Send it back again' I say. Then add, '*My* love. Not the love he sent me, obviously.'

'Of course' he replies, matter-of-factly.

That's the third or fourth quippy little thing I've said in the last few minutes, but there's hardly been a glimmer of recognition in Barry's eyes, nor a trace of irony in his replies.

But just then he leans forward and comes to the point, elbows on desk, hands folded like he's about to read the news.

'Your Edinburgh show was funny too, Jerome . . . have you got any other ideas?'

Other ideas? I'd been putting that together for two years, so no I haven't. But I can't say that to him, a top TV exec.

'Loads' I lie.

'Oh excellent, fire away!'

He takes out a notepad and I speak before I think.

'Something about er, living in a . . . crane.'

'Uh-huh. What happens with the crane then?' he says stifling an unlikely chortle.

Unfortunately, when I started the word 'crane' I didn't actually know what I was going to say. It could just as easily have ended up as 'crate' or 'cranberry juice carton' but now I've got to run with it.

'Well this bloke lives in it and he . . . does stuff. Builds things like . . . like buildings.'

'Mmm.'

'. . . and he has a cat called Ginger, who brings him breakfast.' WHAT AM I DOING!!?

'And they sing songs, sometimes. They're in a band, in fact.'

'A band? Now that's funny' says the Supreme Judge.

'Ginger and the Crane Twins' (Crane twins, sounds like Kray twins, that was lucky.)

'Twins?'

'Yeah, but there's only one.'

'One?'

'That's the joke.'

'Ah-hah, that's funny!'

Idiot. Then he puts his pad down.

'Well why don't you write this up properly and I'll have a look. Then maybe we could work it into a draft and take it to one of the networks. What do you say, mate?' (I use 'mate' too, when I can't remember someone's name.)

'Cool' I say, inexplicably.

Surely he can't think what I've just said was a good idea? I've got lots of others like that. Peter Piffhead and His Amazing Talking Leg, The Ooolerminox Conspiracy, Beetroots Are Humans Too – see I can make them up all day long. Or maybe, just maybe I've stumbled on something brilliant!? Maybe my comedy subconscious, when put under pressure, has thrown up something of pure genius about a man and a cat living in a crane.

No. Definitely not. This bloke is either just humouring me or he's a fool and I don't want anything to do with him. There'd be a long way to go anyway – drafts, re-writes, meetings, lunches, pilots. First nights, chat shows, BAFTA award ceremonies. Calm down.

But what if idiots staff the networks too? It might actually get on TV! Yes. No, it's crap! But surely this man is paid an enormous salary – he should know what he's talking about. He's just got a second series for Penny Bennett. Precisely, that's terrible.

Come on, this is the cocaine-fuelled hothouse of television where anything can get made if you have enough contacts and self-belief.

We carry on chatting about who else is doing what, with lots of 'Have you seen?' and 'Did you like?' But each time I wait for his lead before venturing an opinion.

'Do you know . . .' such and such a programme he says.

'Yes – remarkable' I reply ambiguously. And if I don't know the person he mentions at all I say '. . . I think I know the name' not wanting to look off the pace. But at least twice he looks unnervingly directly at me and says 'Well, I've heard good things . . .'

But I wonder if he has. He's probably heard one 'good thing'. Or just, 'a thing'. He's another chameleon who somehow seems to have the power to make me want to change my skin colour as well. He probably didn't even see my Edinburgh show. Everyone he knows is either 'lovely' or 'a bastard'. No in-betweens. What am I? A fraud. Come on, be yourself.

That's it! He hasn't got a sense of humour has he? I don't believe it – one of the judges in the beauty contest is as blind as a bat. He doesn't get my jokes; he probably doesn't get anyone's jokes, all his opinions are ratings driven. Incredible.

I should've told him my other idea of a young writer who has had so many knock backs he takes a TV producer hostage in his office, and then threatens to behead him live on the news unless he's allowed to read out his sitcom. That would wipe the grin off his mask.

Just then I notice the tassels on his shoes. Two little leather pom-poms sitting meekly on top of his tan moccasins. I take this as a sign of weakness, and decide to express some of my own thoughts.

'Is Penny going to finish each episode with a song like she did in the last series? I'm not sure it works.'

'That was my idea' squeaks Barry in his best 'I'm so hurt' voice.

'I could be wrong' I add hastily.

Just then Farah comes in to tell him his 12.15 is here. An appointment I suppose, not a train. (Perhaps he presses a button under his desk to terminate an interview he's not enjoying any more.)

'We'll be in touch soon' he says.

Yup, he's withdrawing himself with the speed of a retractable plug into a vacuum cleaner. He extends a hand without looking at me. He'll get Farah to phone.

'Cool' I say again, to my increasing horror. I didn't realise it was infectious. Now I've got a whole rash of them – 'cool sores'.

'Your taxi's here' says Farah.

'Cool' I reply helplessly.

She shows me back down the walk of fame, and then I stride across the foyer and straight into the glass door. Farah giggles and I do a Stan Laurel face to pretend it was deliberate. (You see I can make people laugh alright, it's just I don't know where or when.)

I leave depressed that the Supreme Judge of Funny is so far out of touch with public opinion. Or is he? Need to get home, watch some *Fawlty Towers* videos and re-set my laughter gauge.

I've had a few of this type of depressingly baffling meetings now, and it's slowly dawning on me that the talent behind the scenes is just as hit and miss as the talent in front. Their problem, of course, is that the gold they are looking for is not gold until someone else says it is, sometimes after a second or third series.

In the end I pay the fare, get out and walk. But not before the driver has pressed that special button which rounds it up to a random number well above the one showing.

Barry never sees a draft of 'Ginger and the Crane Twins'. But not long after he goes on to be the controller of a whole TV station. Now that's funny.

Ice

January 1997: A cable car going down to Chamonix

Completely exhausted and mentally destroyed. My wife's ex has just rescued me from the top of a mountain and now I'm stuck in a cable car with him.

A little comedy tour of ski resorts in the French Alps for well-off kids and Brits abroad. Not good money but free skiing for three days. Then Marita discovers some old university friends will be in Chamonix around the same time so she comes along, and we leave our delightful monkeys with my parents.

The novelty of a white vista can cheer up any dreary winter, as well as the promise of hot food and fortified drink, to offset the icy chill. The audiences are good-willed but tire towards the end of the shows as the day's exertions catch up with them.

I knew it was him straight away – Klaus the ski instructor. Tanned face, smaller than I imagined, a twinkle in his eye. He hugs Marita close as if he's familiar with her body. Or did I just imagine that? We're introduced. But that's as far as it goes. Somehow we both make sure that our eyes never meet, or that we're found in the same conversation. I should try and be a grown up about this.

The eight members of Heidelberg University's class of '89 meet the day after my shows finish. Just as well they don't see me perform perhaps, because although over the years Marita has warped to my way of thinking, maybe her friends when faced with something as bare-faced as a pun, would be more likely to conform to the German stereotype.

'Ah, a word with two meanings. Not amusing, but very efficient!'

But I do feel strangely undressed without a gig to justify my presence – now I'm just 'Marita's English husband'. They've heard what I do, but I fear their picture of a comedian is of a fat man in lederhosen hitting another fat man in lederhosen over the head with some kind of sausage.

Also, feeling slightly threatened and surrounded by German voices stirs up all my oldest prejudices. In the bar that night I'm an English spy surrounded by Waffen SS. I imagine digging a tunnel like in *The Great Escape*, and releasing soil from my trousers every time I visit the Gents.

But in truth Marita's friends are tolerant and multilingual, androgynous even, with earrings and hair lengths that blur the line of the sexes. I feel uptight and immature by comparison. These are modern Germans who have each found a niche in European society – professors, writers, social workers, oh and a ski-instructor. (Has he moved on I wonder?)

But I don't think of Marita as being one of them, she's a double agent who defected long ago. Yes it was me who turned her on to the thrill of the useless male. All it takes is 'a look' here and a codeword there for us to communicate virtually unnoticed. She could never go back. Although somehow it seems she's really enjoying herself.

But fascism is alive and well on the slopes. You can either ski or you can't, and never has a mode of travel been combined so well with showing off. If only there was some way of bringing them all down to earth. (In *The Great Escape* didn't Steve McQueen procure a motorbike by tying a wire between two trees?) Well, it's just that sometimes it all seems like a lot of trouble to just go 'Weeeee!' down a hill.

They're all good skiers and want to go up to the Vallee Blanche on their first day, the most picturesque but difficult route. My German is nicht gut, and my skiing's worse. I try to tell them this, but both facts somehow seem to cancel each other out.

The next morning we all clamber into a big red box and whirr up into the sky. Marita is full of a cold and gives it a miss. (Why didn't I think of that?) We're all clumped together in our fluorescent Gortex each with our own armoury of thin bits of metal. Then it's all change and into another cable car. And another. Up and up the mountain, we must be quite near the moon now. It's a lot chillier up here than it is down below. Now we follow a tiny path along the side of a sheer drop, holding on to only a rope. A three thousand feet drop they say. So now I'm about three thousand feet out of my depth then.

Off the path, and before us is a huge bright white tablecloth over an upturned table, with lots of craggy legs. There's a lot of fresh snow and it's a steep start. The others go on. I manage to ski a few hundred metres then fall over. It's a horrendous effort to get back on my skis. Then I'm down again. Now I've lost a ski. It's almost impossible to put it on in all this snow. At last I manage it. And fall again. Klaus has instinctively turned back. Why him? Perhaps he has a Luger pistol in his pocket and he's come to finish me off.

'Nein nein, put zis foot in here . . .'

I fall at his feet. This is truly pathetic. Perhaps I should wrestle him to the ground and slit his throat. I'm hot and tired and close to tears but trying not to show it. It's no good.

'You can't go on, it's too dangerous.'

He gets out his phone, and tells the others. Now he makes another call. He is speaking fluently in French. 'Helicoptaire'!? I definitely heard him say that word. Anything but that! I'd rather jump off the edge than have the humiliation of being airlifted off the mountain for nothing more than incompetence.

'It's okay' I say, desperate. 'I'll walk back.'

'It's a long way back in deep snow.'

He looks towards the direction of the others. They've long gone. 'Come on I will go back with you.'

I would say 'no' but then again I might just die out here. Yeah and then he might fancy his chances with Mrs Stevens again. He leads the way uphill, me planting my feet in the holes his have made. It's about five hundred metres in drifts of snow of a couple of feet deep, on the edge of the world. After an hour we've done about a third of it. We lie down hot and shattered. Some skiers come the other way and ask if we need help. Klaus explains and they just shake their heads.

So this is the difference between making an audience laugh and being the laughing stock. It certainly didn't happen in 633 Squadron did it? – the mission fails because the reconnaissance party fell off their skis and couldn't get them back on again.

'Don't worry, I did this with my son once' he confides.

I don't know whether to be happy or sad – it implies that my skiing is no better than a child's – but he has a son! That means he *has* moved on then.

'How old is your son?'

'Seven years now.'

Again I feel two things at once. His son was probably only a baby when he had to turn back with him, but then another part of my brain does an insane calculation to check that Marita didn't have a baby she hasn't told me about. It's okay, she couldn't have. Now I feel bad for doing the sum.

But suddenly Klaus doesn't seem so threatening after all. A decent chap with an easy smile, I can almost see what she saw in him.

'You are a comedian, Ja?'

'Can't you tell by the way I ski?'

He laughs.

'You should come to a show' I offer, sincerely. I would genuinely like him to see me occupy a position of much higher status.

'Ja, for sure.'

Now we have to get back along the narrow ridge with the drop. This would be the time I would kill me if I were him. As we turn the corner we're hit with the full force of the wind, which freezes us to the bone. It's a lot harder going back up than it was coming down, when we were full of energy and optimism. A twist in the path, another hundred metres.

At last we're back in the cable car. Both of us are slumped on the floor looking up at the postcard panoramas passing the windows on fast forward, as we shoot back to earth. Both too tired to speak. Well I am.

'We made it Jerome. Well done.'

I don't think he's being patronising. Or perhaps I should ask him to step outside?

Just then he begins to laugh. 'What would Marita say if she could see us?'

'Yeah' I say wondering what he means.

Is it just relief, or is he laughing because the only woman he ever loved has preferred to spend her life with an idiot? Nevertheless he carries on laughing. (In *Where Eagles Dare* didn't Richard Burton fight a German on top of a cable car?)

'Things could be different, Ja?' he ventures.

Yes, I think he does mean Marita and all that. His sigh is rueful enough. Maybe he even has a sense of irony.

'We English have a word for it' I explain. 'Schadenfreude.'

'Surely that is a German word' he says.

'I know. Yeah, I know.' Maybe he doesn't.

Prison ⊞ III

I wonder what my agent is doing about all this? Nothing I expect. Mostly because he won't know yet. I wish I'd been nicer to him now, it's just you don't want to get too close. He's an escort to a party and you don't want him getting the wrong idea – that you might spend the rest of your lives together. If you keep a certain distance, then you won't have to kiss him goodnight or if it comes to it, dump him in person.

Now, if I'd gone with Telestar they would've arranged for some mercenaries to come and rescue me in a helicopter. Then they'd have sold the film rights to Tom Cruise. Either that or take the whole cost of the mission out of all my future earnings. Yes, more likely they'd have kept me in prison if it would sell more DVDs! Next time I speak to Gordon I'll definitely ask him if he's got any kids or something. If I ever get to speak to anyone again, that is.

Deceptive Bend

A family atmosphere. Pensioners and tourists. It's not often I'm on the tube in the middle of the day, but it's still a crush. You should be able to pay extra and then get to drive the train yourself. Or if a particular train is late three days running you should get to keep it.

I could be in an advert! But I only have 24 hours to learn the script.

'Mmm that's lemony!'

Learnt it, excellent. I really don't know why actors go on about learning lines. I'm on my way to a casting for an ad for a new carpet cleaner.

'Mmm that's lemony!' Yes, I think I can manage that alright. It pays thousands, probably.

I get up to Soho for 10.30. At 11 I'm still sitting in the design agency amongst a dozen 30-something quirky blokes who all, disconcertingly, look a bit like me. We've been told to fill in some forms and have our Polaroids taken. I've done these a few times before. They're dead easy. Mind you I've never got the part yet.

The first one I ever went to, I was late. The train got stuck in a tunnel. I ran into the waiting room covered in sweat. Spaz happened to be there already, and managed to size up the situation pretty quickly.

'In you go mate' he said, handing me a script. 'It's an advert for cheese crackers, they want a loud German accent, really over the top.'

Fantastic, I thought, I'll just pretend to be Marita's Uncle Bernhardt. I glanced at the script and gave it my biggest Bavarian. But the four execs and cameraman just looked at me open-mouthed, until one of them coughed and said 'thank you very much'.

Back in the waiting room Spaz was crying full length on the floor, and several others I didn't know were laughing too. It was actually an appeal for money on behalf of orphans in Africa. (I wondered why £12 a month would make a difference with regard to savoury biscuits.)

This morning it was all commuters. I was young and ambitious then. The floor of this train is made of wood, like the deck of a ship. This afternoon I've been cast adrift with the women and children.

Over there, one of the 'me's is talking to another 'me'. Except they're not like me in that they're bubbly and full of life. I have a headache; I was in Lincoln last night and got home after three. They're all swapping stories about how there's not much work about, and how casting directors never know what they want. They seem to me, like typical actors, the sort you'd cast in a sitcom to play unemployed actors. I wonder how long ago they last worked together? Last Christmas demonstrating toys in Hamleys? Or maybe in the summer as extras at the London Dungeon.

But as I'm thinking disparaging thoughts, I'm treated to a superb display of genuine acting, because just then, what must be the casting director, walks in.

'Brian! how are you mate!' says the first actor.

'. . . er . . . Jimmy' says the director eventually recognising him, 'I didn't know you were up for this.'

'Wouldn't miss it for the world, do you know Ralph Peters?' he says, introducing another 'me'.

'Don't think I do. Brian Lorrenzo' says the director.

'Pleasure to meet you Brian, loved the thing you directed for Granada, by the way' says the immediately obsequious Ralph.

'Oh thanks very much' replies Brian, won over.

See how they're working as a team, like a pack of hyenas. Now it's Jimmy's turn.

'You're looking great Brian, old buddy. How's Linda?'

'Lottie?'

'Yes, Lottie, that's right.'

'Good, really good, thanks, just had a baby.'

'Oh congratulations mate!! So not getting much sleep then!'

'It's not too bad actually. Last night we got seven hours. She slept . . .'

'. . . like a baby!' roars Ralph.

When the chuckling dies down, Brian gets back to business. 'Er . . . right who am I seeing next?'

Amazing that, they both changed from hangdog losers into the sort of bright-eyed Labrador anyone would want as their best man, and all at the drop of a name. I'm not sure if my opinion of them has just gone up or down.

South Kensington: yuk, a party of school children have got on. What a racket, enough of that at home, I'll change carriages.

That's the difference between actors and stand-ups. Actors are more dependent on others for work and have to be enthusiastic, write begging letters, and generally act professionally. Stand-ups don't bother. They tend to think that the world is lucky to hear them speak. This means they get to work on their own a lot. Actors often venerate stand-ups. They say things like 'I could never do that. Oh you're so brave.'

But most stand-ups are indifferent to actors, partly because they say things like that, but also because, to them, they always seem to ride with stabilisers – a script and without the possibility of unplanned interaction between them and the crowd. Although, stand-ups who get to try any proper acting are often horribly surprised by the teamwork and accuracy required.

It's Jimmy's turn to go and visit his old mate Brian to do his little audition. From time to time we can hear muffled shouts, of 'now that's lemony' coming out of the room.

Now *that's* lemony!

Now that's *lemony*!

Now that's lemony!

The rest of us roll our eyes in a sort of 'I wish the guy getting electrocuted wouldn't scream so much, given that we're next' sort of a way.

After 10 minutes Jimmy brazenly steps through the door without mentioning 'the noises'. He sidles up to Ralph and mentions something about meeting up for a drink sometime. I picture them both at a roadside café with a bottle of 7Up. Then they both take a sip and exclaim together 'Now *that's* lemony!'

They both wish each other good luck, then Jimmy goes out into the day to get on with the rest of his resting, I suppose.

Oh yes, when you leave an audition like this you must forget about the whole thing. Keep your eyes steadfastly on being rejected. You may get a second audition, but don't let them torture you by spending the money in your head. You never get as much as you think anyway.

The people you see in ads, posters, newspapers, and magazines – they all got chosen like this – their stupid faces captured forever. A lie for posterity. But then perhaps they all have little mouths to feed, little mouths that start singing at half past six in the morning.

My turn.

'Can you speak to the camera and tell us your name and agent.'

'Jerome Stevens, Gordon Heath.'

'And have you done any other commercials for floor cleaners in Denmark?'

(Oooh, now let me think.)

'No.'

I don't have any adrenaline for this. It's just speaking to two men in a room and one of them's behind a camera. No audience to time anything off.

'Right can you just pick up the product and say the line. But quite naturalistically, not too cartoon-like. Genuine, but with a hint of surprise.'

'Er, okay.'

'Right and . . . action!'

'Now that's Melanie!'

Heavy Plant Crossing

July 1997: Newport to London by walking briskly then car

'We've gotta get out of this place, if it's the last thing we ever doo...'

The radio is now at full volume as I race towards the Severn Bridge, and it bellows out exactly what I'm thinking. It's certainly the nearest thing to luck I've had this evening.

When a show begins it's as if each person in the crowd is a pixel on a TV screen. If you're winning them over they can begin to take on the form of something friendly – a compliant pet or even an old friend you can have a chat with. Other times the picture falters as reception comes and goes, and then occasionally the whole thing just blows up in your face and leaves you picking bits of glass out of your hair for months to come.

You see, you can unlock a room by how you interact with the crowd. It gives them faith, if they see you deal with things off the cuff. If there's any trouble you just make an example of someone, that's all. No need to unleash Hiroshima, just take out a small, uninhabited island so that everyone knows where they stand.

I must have got a bit complacent then. It was going so well. A corporate for 250 brewery staff in Newport.

'Bit odd this' I quip. 'Here you are on your night off with free food and drink – surely you get that every night of the week?'

'We don't get free food and drink' a female voice pipes up.

'Then how come you're all so fat?' says I, the comedian. Except at that moment, suddenly I'm not a comedian anymore.

There's an audible gasp.

'. . . What I meant . . .' I say, playing for time.

But now I've become a callous stranger who has just insulted Margaret from Accounts; brave Margaret who has battled for years with obesity, although I only begin to realise this as she and her horizontally challenged support group walk, well waddle, out of the room.

Some drunk lads at the back fail to disguise their cackling. Others respond to this with tuts and boos. Struggling, I try to win them round with my holiday stuff. But I don't. No one's listening now. People are beginning to talk and others are leaving the room, like ice breaking off a melting iceberg.

Behind me the sky is dark. Billowing satanic clouds full of griffins, warlocks and angry miners, who probably streamed out of the pits early, the moment they heard about the unprovoked attack on poor Margaret.

'Before I go I have something for you . . .' I say.

The room falls quiet for a second. With hindsight a few fair-minded people might have been expecting some kind of an apology. Probably not the '. . . CONTEMPT!' I shout before stumbling off the stage to no applause at all.

It was a put-down rehearsed for a different sort of angry crowd. Now the picture on the screen has gone forever, now it's just a bunch of angry pixels fizzing about like mental Rice Krispies. Not so much a death as an assisted suicide.

But this is only the beginning. Afterwards, large men with valley accents surround me. Big red-eyed bruisers with shaking heads, stubby accusing fingers and tattoos smudged by years of acid rain.

'She's in pieces in the other room, crying!'

My stomach turns over, as suddenly there's the familiar threat of violence in the air. The fruit machines in the foyer chirp into action, they'll entertain without insulting you.

'Go and apologise, it's the least you can do!'

'After all she's been through . . .'

I make my excuses and prepare to leave by a back exit.

'I can only give you half your money. You only did half your time' says the weasely promoter. I'm not in a position to argue.

'Should I go and apologise?' I say hoping he won't want an actual murder in his club.

Reg does a thing these days when he doesn't really want to say sorry. He says 'sorop' – almost the right word but not quite. This is how I feel. I didn't know what she'd been through. Yes, the best I can manage is a big fat 'sorop', as it were.

'Run to the car!' says the promoter as he stuffs a wedge of tenners into my hand.

'Run!? run?' I won't be intimidated. I walk, briskly.

Now I have to stop for petrol. But I didn't really want to have to do this in Wales; I'd prefer to get across the bridge. What if they've sent out a posse on pit ponies? What if they've phoned ahead to every services from here to London? I'll buy a Twix to cheer me up.

But I can't help replaying the moment in my mind again and again, each time remembering another gruesome detail. She had two old people with her. Were they her parents? It wasn't my fault! I didn't know she was in the audience! Anger swells up, it wasn't my fault. I don't want to think about her pain – the rejection, the tears, the soul eroding ridicule. Yes, she's had a lot on her plate, stop it, just stop it!

There's a long queue of customers underneath the bright lights of the garage shop. Now there's a large egg-shaped man behind me with a fist-full of coloured chocolate bars. Perhaps he's a relative. I make a mental note of where the automatic glass door is – and I'm pretty confident of getting there before he does. (Is it just me, or are all automatic doors set a bit too slow, so that you have to break your stride whatever speed you're doing?)

Now I'm over the river, I've crossed the Styx and am back in the land of the living. Just before crossing, I misread a sign. 'Troll Bridge', I thought it said, and imagined another large relative straddling the lanes, having caught wind of family trouble.

I sing along with every song that comes on the radio, read out-loud every signpost. I'm trying to forget.

'Like a bridge over troubled water – ah Swindon!' Whose inhabitants, of course, are known as 'swine'. Certainly to anyone who's played the Green Cat Café there! Ha ha it's not just in Wales that I can be offensive!

Of course, I've done bad gigs before. It makes you want to forget, to drink or take something that dulls the pain. You've embarrassed yourself and you need to become someone else, quick! Time will help, but only a really storming gig will take away the memory.

It doesn't always go wrong. Sometimes it goes fantastically right. Yes, like that night in Brixton when I picked on those Swedish people. They ended up singing the whole of 'I Wanna Be Like You' from *The Jungle Book* in Swedish – much to the joy of the rest of the room. Somehow I seemed to get the credit for making it happen. That was a good night.

Even now, slowly, the more distance I put between me and this evening, well, the more distance I seem to put between me and this evening. Tonight the arrows almost found the chinks in my armour.

'How come you're all so fat?!'

I surprise myself by laughing out loud.

The truth is, I like this job. Since Edinburgh my diary's filled right up. I'm not so shy anymore, the other day I did a phone interview on a crowded train for goodness sake. Once you scramble up the sheer cliff-face, there's a nice big plateau on top. I enjoy it and I know I can be good at it, possibly really good. In time this will just be another well-worn story, slowly dropping down the charts of my top 10 anecdotes.

Yes, this is my job. It turns out my teachers at school were wrong about me. These days I get to stay up late and buy as many sweets as I like. My adolescent worries have all but disappeared – of not amounting to anything, not being interesting enough, not having sex before the world ends, or whatever. Now, I have licence to bully the bullies back. Licence to kill or be killed. Sure, there might be a bit of collateral damage from time to time – a stray bullet, which is I suppose more likely to hit some people than others.

I've reached Reading. Made famous by Otis Reading of course. Yes. You often see him sitting by the dock of the . . . mini roundabout. Then I whistle the whistle at the end of the song. People often whistle when they're embarrassed about something. I'm not embarrassed. I refuse to be.

'How come you're all so fat?!'

I say it again. What was I thinking? I laugh again. I'll dine off this one. And on my Twix. Two fingers to the lot of them.

Sheer Drop

October 1997: Limousine to Cheltenham
'Did you get Sean Connery's Christmas card?'

'Did you get Sean Connery's Christmas card?'

Freddie McKay is a TV star, and let's just say he moves in different social circles to me. He presents a game show on ITV that gets huge ratings and I'm supporting him on tour. On stage he has a camp charisma that can be both engaging and offensive all in the same sentence.

He's been a household name for about five years now, but the ratings of his show *Gone for a Ducky* are suddenly on the slide. Last month a Sunday paper published an out of focus photo of him putting the bins out under the caption, 'Freddie looks for better jokes'.

He's always getting me and Jane, the stage manager, to go into hotel foyers, restaurants and theatres before he does, just to pat the place down for journalists. But he's also furious with the Press for beginning to exclude him from the style pages of the glossy magazines.

He's also having boyfriend trouble. He has four you see, two in Britain and one each in Australia and Canada. A sailor in every port, but one of them has found out about another. Freddie says he's keen to do the right thing and is asking our advice. I'm not sure I can help.

He is likeable though. He has an endearing vulnerability that makes you want to look after him, although sometimes he can be quite hard work.

The seats are cream leather and comfortable. The conversation revolves around Freddie and if he doesn't like a turn it takes, he just cuts across and steers it back his way.

We've just been for a large Thai meal that Freddie insisted on, even though he said he wasn't hungry. Now we're on our way to Bristol tonight because Freddie doesn't like the hotels in Cheltenham.

Even off stage he maintains his repertoire of mannered tics. The engaging smile, a pat on the knee, a self-conscious biting down on the bottom lip and then his signature 'Ohh that could be construed as something else' face. His skin is still faultless, although his neck is just beginning to look a bit more tortoise-like, and gives away his 50-odd years (I'm guessing).

Now we have to stop. Freddie is hungry again.

'Don't be silly, you've just eaten!' I'd say if he were a spoilt child of mine. No chance of telling him off though, we all want to hitch a lift on this bandwagon for as long as possible.

His audience isn't really my sort of crowd, but the shows are going all right. Warm up acts are like that – you want someone who's going to do well, but not that well. Someone solid but who doesn't step on your territory. Well, I didn't think they were my audience, but last night after the show there was a middle-aged man in a pullover waiting at the stage door.

'Freddie won't be out for a couple of minutes' I say breezing past.

'It's *you* I want' he says. Then he gives a little laugh.

'Er', I'm taken a back.

'Pretty please!' Then there's that laugh again.

'Oh right.'

He has tonight's programme open on the page with my tiny photo.

The pen doesn't work.

'This pen doesn't seem . . .'

Then it does.

'The surprise element!' he chortles.

Then it stops again.

'Ah . . . no problemo!'

He opens his jacket and there are five or six pens neatly clipped to his inside pocket.

'Like a scout – always prepared!'

I anticipate his chortle, and this time can't help joining in.

'Nice set' he adds, self-consciously using the terminology of stand-up.

'Thanks, who's it to?'

'Alfie.'

'Didn't do the routine about tigers tonight did you?' he says.

'No, it's a bit old – trying to drop it now.'

'Turning over new material eh!'

'That's right.'

'Night, see you in Bristol' he adds. Then the laugh again.

Now I make my way to the car park with the rest of the audience. Normally I keep my head down because I'm only the support act. This time I keep it down in case I meet another Alfie. Not that I'm not pleased, in a way. Won't bother mentioning it to Freddie though.

Jane's got on to some gossip about someone only she and I know. Freddie cuts across saying he wants to get some sleep as he's got to see the Duke of Gloucester tomorrow about a polo pony! Of course he has.

It's a glimpse into a different world – his friends, his attitude and what he spends his money on. He's on show all the time, but then he did apply for the post of specimen in a jar (as indeed I have, I suppose).

It's strange, because I remember Freddie before his success, when he was topping the bill and I was just starting out. He was good, but not that good – not necessarily someone you'd have marked out for stardom. Sometimes his charm would just fall flat. I remember him throwing a microphone stand at a stag night when one of them playfully called him a 'big poof'. But he always does well now – now that he doesn't have to win anyone over.

'That was really brave, starting the way you did' he said in the restaurant after the show.

'What do you mean?' I said.

'That racial thing you did, what was it you said? "Oh – I've heard of the Cheltenham races, but looking round it seems to be mainly white people."'

It was a risky start that didn't really ingratiate me to an unsure audience, but Freddie appreciated its edginess. He does 'edgy' but only in a risqué sense. His audience probably wouldn't let him do anything political. I get the impression he'd quite like to drop all the innuendo and faux outrageousness and talk about something else. He used to have loads of material about avoiding paying the rent, and Club 18-30's. But now he owns three houses – in London, New York and Marrakech – and most people won't identify with a routine that starts 'You know when you're looking for staff abroad . . . ?'

He always seems to be in need of constant reassurance. About his jokes, his perfume and his new pointy snakeskin shoes. But then he does have to sign countless autographs and is constantly being asked to do things for charity – gigs, donating stuff for auctions, kissing babies and literally having the disabled wheeled in front of him to receive his blessing.

Of course he always obliges. But like me, he still appears to be waiting for just the right break. Perhaps that never changes. I mean good luck to him, but how far removed from ordinary life do you have to be, to ask someone you don't know too well if they got Sean Connery's Christmas card? And what's the correct answer. Is it a) I got Roger Moore's and Pierce Brosnan's but Sean's must have got lost in the post; b) Oh I don't speak to Sean, not since the kilt and the kerosene incident or; c) Freddie, listen I've never even met Sean Connery and if you don't get some help or at least some real friends you're probably going have some sort of breakdown.

After a while I just say 'Er, no, don't think so'. And then make a mental note to use it as an example when telling people how far he's lost touch with reality.

Slowly we all nod off as the limo swishes along the M32 to Bristol. 'Bristol'? Hang on; didn't that bloke Alfie say 'See you in Bristol'?

Prison IIII IIII

At first you think that destiny will come knocking on your door. But it turns out that in order to succeed you have to go to hers, and keep on knocking even when she pretends not to be in.

No doors opening here.

Sure, it makes you hard. You have to be.

This stillness is quite unnerving. Usually, whatever's happening, my mind is already on to the next joke, the next show, the next door that could open. But here I don't know what's next. I don't know if I want to know either. Of course I'm used to being on my own. Travelling. Facing down an audience. I have to be, so that I can mentally step aside to analyse words, behaviour and events, and then report back to the crowd. This time I might not get that chance.

Live Rail

Marita and I are gliding through London. The lights are bright, and for tonight anyway, I'm a TV star. But it so nearly all went wrong. Don't want to think about it now – it was all a bit traumatic. But the tape keeps running in my head again and again.

It's my first slot on a TV show, and it's a big one. *Big Night Out* is broadcast live on BBC 2 at 10.40 on Friday nights. This means there won't be any re-takes, as we call it in the biz, I expect. TV! This is it! Everyone has a television. Can't ask to get off the runaway train now. Seven minutes for the equivalent of two hundred pizzas. Lovely.

A car picks me up and drops me at the studio, although actually it would have been quicker to get there by tube. A chauffeur driven limousine! (Mercedes – frighteningly confident.)

I'm met by a runner who introduces me to lots of people, all with different jobs, whose names I instantly forget. Eventually I meet the producer. I know he's important.

'Lovely to meet you Jerome.'

He knows my name!

We're taken down to the studio, which is a huge room about the size of a small department store. Lots of cameras, wires and people with headphones all facing lots of banked up seats for tonight's audience. I try to look nonchalant, like a cricketer inspecting the pitch before a match. 'Hmm this room should take observational comedy pretty well' I think. 'Start with a bit of pace, then bring on the yarn-spinners . . .'

'Get off the floor unless you're needed please' shouts one of the bossy people I was introduced to earlier.

Just going. She can't have realised who I am, surely.

The car is taking all sorts of short cuts – didn't know about that one. Must make a mental note for next time I'm round here. If I ever drive to a gig again, that is. Probably will. I'm at the Demented Chicken for sixty quid on Tuesday.

There's a run through in the early afternoon.

'It's just a camera rehearsal' says the runner who's guiding me to the stage.

Then I say, 'What – to check you've got film in?'

He laughs. Everyone must say that though. That's the sort of thing a 'funny uncle' says to a wedding photographer, for goodness sake.

We get to my bit in the rehearsal.

'Ladies and Gentlemen, Jerome Stevens!'

The Floor Manager claps slowly to convey applause, but to me it sounds like he's just being sarcastic. I come out past the flimsy looking set and take the mic. There are the crew and all the good-looking boys and girls, employed to fill the first few rows of the audience.

What is it about models? Large symmetrical features and that disinterested, 'I don't talk to you, you talk to me' expression. But if you do actually talk to them, they often seem to have a tiny personality, like a jockey driving a Rolls-Royce.

'Action!' says the director.

'Good evening . . .' I say. Then there's a pause.

'Just do the jokes you're doing tonight' says a disembodied voice.

'Um do I have to . . . ?' I plead.

'Well, what are you ending on?'

'Um, the Geordie Dragon thing.'

'What are the last words?'

'Um . . . hang on . . . Geordie . . . er . . . and I haven't been up North since!'

'Okay . . . let's move on.'

Although it might not have looked like it exactly, I'd forgotten my words, horribly. My intention was to run through my lines, but I just had no adrenaline and suddenly my act was well . . . gone! What if that happens in front of several million people tonight? The whole show will grind to a halt and I'll become the startled rabbit who forgot everything – to be shown on TV disaster clip shows ever after.

Back in the dressing room afterwards, running through my lines, it's all there. No! I left a bit out! The clammy wet blanket of fear is descending round my shoulders. It's bad enough when there are one or two people in the audience that you know – you see everything through their eyes. But this moment of truth will be wired direct into the living rooms of all my friends, relatives, neighbours, acquaintances; people I was at school with; people I saw on the bus once; and friends of relatives of people I saw on a bus once; and so on.

Four hours until the show. Now, I keep wanting to swallow. Yes a terrible gulp keeps rising up, even when I'm not thinking about it. Go away.

Now there are just two hours before the show. That was a quick couple of hours! There's a knock at the door. It's the producer. He wants a chat. (Does he know I dried, or has he heard about my no film in the camera quip – and now he's going to throw me off the show?)

He looks like a student, foppish hair, Oxfam cardigan and red shoes. He also never quite looks anyone in the eye. 'Oi I'm over here!' you feel like saying as he talks to the wall. He was probably bullied at school. If not, he should have been. Halfway through our conversation at a right angle to each other, I have a sudden urge to push him across the room. Maybe it's his red shoes.

'Listen fella' he begins, taking on the affected speech pattern of a lorry driver. 'It's just that Pete Pendleton is the act on before you . . . and you look quite similar.'

'So?'

'Would you mind changing your image? Perhaps put on a suit and alter your hair style?'

'Oh right.'

'I'm really sorry to ask you to do this, fella, but it would really help the show.'

Now he looks me in the eye. I offer to think about it. The door shuts.

Now I feel like I'm trapped underneath a huge pile of wood in the late afternoon of November 5th.

No no no no NO! I've spent years putting this act together I can't change it all an hour before a live TV show!

A phone call to Gordon – he's furious. That's nice, normally our relationship is purely utilitarian. Obviously he's a bit tense about this too. That doesn't help. The more I think about what they've just asked, the more ridiculous it seems.

I refuse to change my image. Now the whole world is against me, and everything could be lost in less than seven minutes. This is a battle, but the enemy is within. Pacing up and down, talking to myself out loud.

'Come on, show them what you can do!'

'Your destiny is in your own hands.'

'The only thing you have to fear is (gulp) fear itself.'

Time to go into make-up. Jill takes one look and says 'Do you know, I don't think you need any, love.'

Is this a compliment or part of a conspiracy? Old red shoes has told her not to give me any assistance hasn't he? Or is my skin so bad that she doesn't want anything to do with it? On the credits, make-up will be 'by Jill Maplin (apart from Jerome Stevens who did his own!)'.

I talk her into giving me some powder. Then while she's dib dabbing away I compliment her on her tan. But apparently that comes from having a house in Spain – make-up ladies must get paid more than I thought. She shows me a picture of the villa, and

I imagine her up a ladder filling in last minute cracks before the sun comes out.

We're swooshing past hundreds of homes, occasionally catching a glimpse of a television through one of the windows. I popped up in their living rooms this evening. Well some of them. If I'd seen them all at once, staring back at me from their little homes, on threadbare sofas and slouched on their bean-bags, I'd definitely have forgotten what to say.

Transfixed by the monitor in the green room, I stand, shifting from one foot to the other, as the show unfolds. The set of an exploding spaceship looks surprisingly good on camera, much better than it does from behind.

The first band is on. The bimbos dance along like they've been paid to. Getting them to laugh along is going to be much harder, especially if I forget what I'm going to say, and then swallow myself whole.

The runner comes to take me down to the studio. On set there's plenty of applause and laughter and the MC Roy Bracewell's intros all sound slick, but it's a lot more frantic behind the scenes and occasionally you can hear snatches of more desperate conversations coming out of people's headphones. I'm counted down on the Floor Manager's fingers . . . four, three, two, one . . .

It goes fine. Although I wouldn't say I enjoyed it. I felt peculiarly detached, as if a stunt double was saying the words for me.

Marita comes to the after show party and it's a relief to see a familiar face. We mingle with the pop stars and try not to stare. A couple of times I notice that my arm is a bit stiff, and eventually work out that this is because I was holding the microphone so tightly.

That bloke Alfie from Cheltenham was in the crowd again. Fortunately I didn't see him until afterwards. It would have thrown me otherwise. I'm sure he tried to catch my eye but I disowned him. I thought groupies were supposed to be girly teenagers, not middle-aged men who probably enjoy Dungeons and Dragons?

Slowly I'm getting used to the idea that from time to time in this business you're on your own again, and that it can feel like you're forced to gamble everything you've achieved so far on your next gig.

Now we pass the cinema. Not everyone watched me tonight then. I was just a part of a part of the entertainment on offer this evening. Others were working, or in the pub, at home, talking while I was on even. In fact most people didn't see it at all. It wasn't that big a deal.

A few days later there's a message from Suzy saying she thought I 'looked nice and relaxed'. Of course I was. It's strange, there was a time when she'd have been able to tell that I wasn't, but I guess she's got other things on her mind.

Only after a few weeks can I bear to face a recording of my ordeal, and even then only from behind a cushion. Although it brings back some scary memories, the small screen filters out the highs and the lows so that the whole thing comes across as – not good but not bad either – just *quite* funny. The laughs are all uniform, no real highs or lows. Watching myself is both pleasing and displeasing. I'm funny but not a genius.

We're home. Back to our yellow front door. My 'goodnight' to the driver is cheery and heartfelt, after all the cab's on account. I potter about absent- mindedly filling the dishwasher until Marita appears at the top of the stairs wearing only a towel.

'How about a perfect end to a perfect evening' she says in her best Marilyn Monroe impression, with a slight German accent. Perhaps it's Marlene Dietrich. It doesn't matter. Then I step on some Lego.

Serious Incident

January 1998: Walk home from the Coach and Horses

It's not often I come out of a pub, these days, without having made anyone laugh. But then tonight is my night off. A couple of hours of badminton; then a few beers with Ralph. But he didn't say much, and left before closing time.

Badminton's in an old scout hut that smells of damp and polish. It's a slow-motion skirmish of force and chivalry, to the squeak of trainer and fizz of angry shuttle. Sometimes the shuttle gets lost in the rafters and you have to play a 'let'. Ralph won this evening but I seem to care less than usual.

There's a gentle breeze and there aren't many cars on the roads out here in suburbia. They're all somewhere else. Up town. I wonder who's on at the Lounge tonight? What kind of animal the crowd is? It's not too late, I could get a taxi, pop in. No, I need a night off. But even now I'm feeling twitchy.

Perhaps I should join Workaholics Anonymous – but I'd probably get too involved. I can't stop can I? Sometimes I think I've started to live my whole life as a routine. 'So I walked into the newsagent . . .' I think as I walk into the newsagent. Then I banter with the man behind the counter, deliberately taking what he says 'the wrong way'.

'Hello' he says. 'I don't want a magazine!' I say.

Then I laugh for effect. The laugh of a professional telling him that it's okay to laugh too. Except he doesn't laugh, because he doesn't speak much English – surely that can be the only explanation.

Tomorrow there'll be a yellow sign up outside the shop: 'FUNNY INCIDENT'. I turn and scan the headlines on the bottom shelf, looking at the rest of the world through the window of my hilarious imagination. 'Thousands dead in Bolivia'. Excellent, I can use my earthquake material again.

I used to walk home this way from school. Trying not to step on the cracks in the pavement. These days it's more a case of trying not to step on the crack cocaine . . . what am I talking about? I know almost nothing about crack cocaine. Only what I've learnt from other stand-up routines. I'm sure a lot of the audience laugh just because they think they should as well.

There are some stand-ups I know, however, who experiment long and hard into the night in the name of tax-deductible research. Spaz is going that way. Last I heard he'd disappeared for three nights in Hong Kong, and then arrived back at the hotel with a headache, no money and eventually Chlamydia.

Everyone has material, not just comedians. Stories they tell, jokes they adapt, urban myths people swear happened to someone they know. But most only have about eight anecdotes. Couples share them, and cajole each other into regaling their friends.

'Tell them the one about the . . .'

'No you tell it . . .'

Then there are the raconteurs – the self appointed kings of conversation, who hold court and proclaim the same stories again and again, goaded on by their loyal subjects who watch and listen attentively for any cue to laugh along obligingly.

They can never be outdone, and have heard all your stories plus one. If somehow you manage to prove that the Pope isn't a Catholic, then they will cut across and chip in 'And you know *why* he isn't don't you . . .' They can never be topped, but you can slow them down a bit by saying 'Apparently all conspiracy theories were invented by the CIA to distract attention from what's really happening.' Often these people see professionals as a threat and want to engage you in some kind of a contest.

Anyway, I need to pick up the shredded tatters of my social life.

I wonder why Ralph left early. Shame, I like Ralph, he tells it how it is, he doesn't care about how things come across. Like his front garden with the old fridge in it. I mean we talked – I told him about how badminton is like comedy – that it's about selling dummies and having total commitment. Then I shared a couple of anecdotes myself. Danny Bullen and the angry Norwegian, the drag act and the old man with the nail gun – they're good stories.

Perhaps Ralph's business isn't going that well. Oh yeah, it was great when those lads in the pub recognised me off the telly. Out of the corner of my eye I could see them looking over and pointing. My signature's certainly getting more flash – well it should be, I've practised it enough. Didn't buy those chips though did I – didn't really want them to see me eat. Not sure why.

People have reacted in different ways to my tiny success. Some friends have been a bit offish as if, clearly, I won't want to have anything to do with them anymore, and to be honest they're not helping. Others who were hardly friends have suddenly been in contact and seem to watch my every move in a slightly creepy 'What's he going to do next!?' sort of way. (But where were this lot a few years ago when I was dying on the open spot circuit?)

Then there are complete strangers like my dentist who while I was lying prone to his sharpest instruments announced he'd seen me perform the week before in Dorking – didn't even say if he liked it.

Ralph is solid though. He knows I have a weak backhand and a tendency for racquet abuse. Yeah, I should've asked him about his job. And perhaps I shouldn't have told him how to tell his anecdote better. The one about the faulty sewer – to say the word 'funeral' as the last word in the sentence, to keep the reveal until the last possible moment (see, working even on my night off!).

I seem to be able to carve jokes out of most things now. Reckon that sometime I should try a sentence that's not even a joke, but just has the right rhythm and intonation and see if I can get a crowd to laugh – bet I could. I had Reg in stitches this afternoon when I noticed that Marita's fleecy top was the same colours as the cartoon character Elmer the Elephant. Marita didn't laugh mind, she probably just hasn't seen the programme.

Trees, lampposts, drains. Nothing funny there. But it's good to have a night off. I turn the corner and in the distance a fox scuttles across our road and into a hedge as if on a roller skate. He's out and about doing gigs, doubling up, bringing home the bacon. I salute him – no, I *actually* salute him – I know where he's coming from you see, but he just stares back.

At home, and everyone is in bed. The toys are tucked away and the cereal packets are out for the morning. But I don't feel like turning in and I'm even a bit bored. What was wrong with Ralph? Think I'll pour myself a drink and see what's on telly. (Just like I would if I'd been working in fact.) Then I'll probably end up watching some trashy film on Channel 5, that I can't believe I'm watching, only to realise halfway through that I've seen it before.

I do exactly that, and then fall asleep on the sofa.

.

Prison ⵑⵑⵜ ⵑⵑⵜ

Perhaps stand-up has turned me into a monster – an armadillo sniffing out termites of fun, impervious to the prods and pokes of my family's cries for attention. Marita says I'm more aggressive to strangers as well, seeking out their vulnerabilities. Although, often when they find out what I do, they just roll over.

'I'm afraid to say anything in case you use it one of your skits!'

Too late.

If I were in a different job would I be a better friend, husband, Dad? Will she tell the kids I wonder? Will they see her crying? Will she cry? Or just shrug her shoulders and carry on with the laundry? She's beautiful – my wife. Yes, my wife. My best friend. The way she looks at me. Used to look at me. Where did that all go?

A sudden noise. A plate of brown rice is shoved under the door. Oh. Well, I assume it's brown rice. Maybe it's just old white rice. There! I saw it move. None for me thanks. Who knows what the guards have done to it. But I am quite hungry. I sniff it. But not *that* hungry. It smells suspiciously of . . . nothing. Or rather the stench of this pit overcomes every other whiff.

The metal bunk beds look tastier than that. Instinctively I know what the metal would taste like. Thinking about it, I know pretty much what everything would taste like. Perhaps that's from going round licking everything as a child.

Ah childhood, where everything was safe and warm. In those days prison was for bad people. Well that's me now isn't it? Mustn't think like that. But I'm more Terry Waite than Peter Sutcliffe, surely. Well, apart from that thing with the eyes. I still can't believe . . . perhaps I should be moved to a special unit for the protection of the guards.

Perhaps the rice is drugged. Perhaps there's a two-way screen and I'm being watched by the guards, even now. Perhaps I'm on a TV reality show. Why? What?

I should try and get some sleep – catch up on my jet lag. Can't get to sleep now. I've forgotten the code: the pin number that gets me through the gate and into the field of dreams. A farmyard where there are sheep dogs and puppies in a manger. Now my fantasies are beginning to tumble into nonsense, and slowly I sink into that benign soup of memories. The puppies yawn silently. Their eyes are still closed.

Then a bark! Very loud. I open my eyes. The grill in the door must have popped open with a rasp, because the plate of rice has gone. Chinese restaurants are like that – leave anything for a couple of seconds and it gets whisked away.

Usually by the end of these trips I'm fed up of all the different food. Yeah, you've got to feel sorry for the Chinese. I mean their food's nice – but every night of the week?

Try and get back to sleep. Now I'm hungry! Of course I am. We were going to eat after the show weren't we? We were going to go to the best local restaurant. Perhaps this is it!

Oh just to be back in my hotel room. They say they're soul-less places, but what do you want, a sign saying 'Tim's room' on the door, model aeroplanes on the wall, discarded socks on the floor? Next time, if I ever get to be in a hotel room again, I'll jump up and down on the double bed, on principle, while wearing the dressing gown and slippers, and conducting music from the television with a Toblerone from the mini-bar.

When I think of what I've taken for granted – the meals, the Jacuzzis and the hours of daytime stretching out before me, before just half an hour's reasonably pleasant work in the evening. Others aren't so lucky. The receptionist in the hotel is often the same person when I check in at six, as when I turn in at one, as when I get up at eleven.

The echo of the shutting grill has just about gone now. It's as if it never happened. Was there a plate? Why would I imagine a plate of inedible food arriving and then disappearing? It's only been a few hours, but it feels like I'm beginning to lose my grip. Come on. Hold it together!

Services

I'm in a spaceship with seven Russian prostitutes.

Actually it's a lift, a glass cube shooting up into the clouds to the bar of a hotel on the 35th floor. My stomach drops through my feet and my ears pop. (On the inside, not on the outside, making a nasty mess.) They must be prostitutes; no one else would wear so much make-up and Lycra in Dubai. Their chaperone is an Arab with glasses on a chain round his neck. He looks like a chemist. Perhaps he's delivering a prescription to a wealthy sheikh – well someone's going to get a dose of something.

I'm running late for tonight, I fell asleep this afternoon after curling up in a blanket to escape the chill of the air-conditioning. Home tomorrow. One more gig.

It's hot outside but I've found it difficult to warm to this place. There are Arabs in full robes but even they seem to mix and match with designer labels – Louis Vuitton, Dolce & Gabbana and Calvin Klein (the boy who made a living from his Mum over-labelling his pants). But 80 per cent of the population is from the Indian sub continent and between you and me they haven't got the best jobs.

As we float on up, the numbers above the lift door bleed orange in turn as if slowly catching fire. The others are talking in at least two different languages.

On arrival at the airport, as we waited by the luggage carousel, first up are a solitary pair of swimming trunks. Ha ha, someone's bag must have opened! Now here come some socks, they look like mine – those were my swimming trunks weren't they? People are laughing. Here they all come, a pair of shorts from Millets, a free T-shirt from a Dutch Comedy Festival, my bath bag, at least it hasn't . . . there's my toothbrush.

I'm here with Vince Matthews and Chris Oki. Vince does downbeat one-liners, tiny hand-grenades of joy, where every word and intonation seems to count. Oki is a Canadian stand-up who does a lot of cultural stereotype stuff, and for whom the word 'awesome' is never more than a few seconds away.

'Wow man' he says as a local passes followed by a line of women in traditional dress. 'Look at those Ninjas go.'

He follows them with his head, hands on hips.

'Awesome.'

There she blows. His act finishes with a New York style rap, which always gets a round of applause, but to my mind it's not so much funny, as just words that rhyme. However, he does have a few telling insights on British culture that ring true without being clichéd.

We all get on well though – people's acts frequently have little bearing on personal chemistry.

Dubai seems to be a feeding trough for all kinds of animals. The Brits sit fat and sleek, pecking at flies on the back of the Arab rhinoceros. Many of them came out for a tax-free smash and grab, but are still here long after the getaway car has been clamped and towed away.

Afterwards, the braver members of the audience seek us out. 'I love Britain, but I could never go back' says Mike a chartered surveyor from Surrey. 'These days it's full of foreigners who can't speak English.'

'Yeah, I hate it when foreigners don't learn the language of the country they're in' says Vince with a twinkle in his eye. 'So how's the Arabic going?'

The wife of the promoter meets us at the airport with one of the ubiquitous limousines. She's manicured, self-possessed and charm itself, until the driver takes a wrong turn and then she screams at him as if he's just run over a child. Composing herself, as she seals him off from our world with the electronic window, she explains without irony that 'it's the only language they understand'. (Urdu, more likely.) It seems they get sent back home if they lose their job – that'll be why the service is good then. No hotel seems to have less than five stars, one even has seven – but if you own the Monopoly board you can make up the rules apparently.

The shows are in tennis clubs and private ex-pat venues. Straightforward, like doing gigs in Epsom. This last one is in a function room at the top of the Excelsior Hotel. The audiences have been enthusiastic, as if we're long lost friends reminiscing about the old days. Here the past is literally another country. But they're all keen to sell the life – justify what they're doing.

Jenny is married to a mechanical engineer from Durham. They've been here four years. She loves it. The weather, the social clubs, and 'Oh yeah, sure, the money is a bonus.'

But then she adds 'You don't want to be here in August though, if you go outside it's like having a hairdryer in your face. It can be very incestuous too, you can't do anything without everyone knowing!'

So it's mainly the money then.

Now I can't tell if we're going up or down – if we've nearly reached the top or the cables have snapped and now we're plummeting into a hole deep beneath the desert. When they exhume our tiny compressed coffin and sort out the DNA, the company I'm keeping might raise a few eyebrows among friends. Small consolation.

The buildings are impressive, at least. It's an architect's playground – a sandpit with unlimited Meccano. Streetlights burn all night on virtually unused motorways that stretch miles out into the desert, then begin to peter out before literally just turning into dust. Here, behind the stage-set of the city, the sand is dirty, uneven and flecked with rubble, stretching to the horizon like a giant chocolate chip cookie. The sky is 'sky blue' and the well-watered grass is 'grass green' – the whole place is manufactured. But is that so bad?

Surely no one would miss a Mercedes? Then I could head off down the empty promenade and into the wilderness beyond. Start a new life . . . with a Bedouin girl, olive-skinned and mysterious. We could spend the day eating olives and watching the sun set. She would have an exotic Arabian name . . . Olive, probably.

Both before and after shows we get to sample authentic Japanese sushi, French haute cuisine, Indian gourmet cooking – all in opulent restaurants but with a vacuous Disney-does-another-country sort of a feel. In one bar, the Filipino house band is superb, with a non-stop cavalcade of perfectly rendered covers. But this is as far as their careers can go isn't it? No one will want to hear a song they've written themselves – a ballad about being a third class citizen in a foreign land. I make a point of shaking the bass player's hand, as he passes through the crowd.

'Nice set mate.'

'Thanks man' he mumbles looking the other way. I've done that.

During the day we can do what we like, visit the gold market, jet-ski, go dune bashing on quad bikes – the promoter's wife will send a driver. Every meal is a buffet. Hundreds of dishes spread out like a huge minefield, and a couple of Indian chefs on stand by in case you want something else.

'Do you do Wagon Wheels?' I ask on behalf of Vince at breakfast.

Blank looks of course.

'Wagon Wheel, it's a chocolate biscuit with white marshmallow.'

Vince laughs. Oki just looks on, wanting to join in, but I suppose in Canada Wagon Wheels are just the wheels of wagons.

'How big?' says the chef. Oh no, they're going to try and make it!

'Never mind' I say, backtracking.

Wish I hadn't started this now. We end with a laugh and a handshake.

But only the Westerners need comedy. No clowns for the Arabs. Only the emotionally uptight need light relief. Perhaps I should try and change things from the stage? One night someone heckles unintelligibly.

'Alright, alright . . .' I reply. '. . . no need to shout . . . I'm not your maid.'

That was my attempt to set the captives free, but I can't help feeling that just by being here I'm somehow complicit with the way things are.

They don't like it if you talk about the whores from the stage. No one likes to admit they're here. Ex-pats, hotel management, the police. But the red lights must have all but gone out in Ukraine. There are Chinese, Indian and Ethiopian professionals here too. ('Whore' is a vicious word. A cheap sound with the minimum of effort.)

You can't really look anyone eye to eye in a lift, you're too close. Instead I steal furtive glances in the mirrors on the walls. Three are tall and leggy, bleached hair with black roots. Bright skin-tight dresses, bangles, tattoos. I try to feel pity, but it doesn't take long before I'm wondering what they would do and for how much.

The other night we met some young American girls down by the pool. They were tanned and lively in a Californian 'anyhoo' sort of way. Chris Oki chatted them up and I watched from a sun lounger shaking my head, and then had to leave when he actually started doing his rap.

'It's like a sauna in here' he says bursting wild-eyed into the sauna where I'd retreated, even though it was the same temperature as outside. He laughs and swears, having just been propositioned by one of them. He wouldn't have minded but they were on the game too, working their way through college. 'High class ho's' as he put it. Everyone's at it! These aren't victims trafficked by ruthless pimps, but just greedy kids, who can't wait to auction themselves.

But my colleagues in the elevator are battle-hardened, with sunken cheeks and eye-sockets thick with mascara. All of us seem to be looking at the floor or the ceiling. Just then someone farts. There are giggles. The tall one tuts. Someone else snorts a laugh. Even their chaperone is smiling. As long as they don't think it's me. No – one of them has gone red. They have some shame! They've been reduced, no elevated, to just giggling girls. Sisters, mothers, daughters.

'Ping'.

Time's up! The hi-tech pod has arrived a quarter of a mile into the sky. The moment has gone. The doors glide apart, and for a second it's as if we've all just appeared on a stage in the corner of a room. A murmur of conversation in the place starts up again. (It must have stopped.) One of us giggles. We must look like a dodgy band in the Eurovision Song Contest. Abdul, me and our crazy backing group.

The lounge is plush with low chairs, concealed lighting and a pianist playing Gershwin. Abdul curses and presses the 'close door' button. The doors shut. We're off again. But the numbers on the dial aren't moving. I'm stuck at the back. It's too late to get out. Where are we going?

'Ping'.

This time it sounds more sinister.

The doors scroll back to reveal a busy room perspiring loud rock music. The girls immediately step out of the lift and get to work. Various Arabs and Europeans are lolling about on piles of cushions surrounded by coffee tables with bottles of spirits and piles of white powder on them. At one end of the room a girl in a few shreds of leather is writhing about in a metal cage suspended from the ceiling. No one is watching her. Well apart from me now.

'Mayday, mayday' I think, but turning back I see the lift is guarded by two Slavic looking heavies. One has the handle of a gun clearly sticking out of his pocket. Perhaps it's just a handle. Doubt it. Would it be quicker, I wonder, to jump off the balcony?

Stepping outside it's suddenly warm, like walking face first into the lagged boiler of an airing cupboard. You can't even see the ground for heat haze. The glittering Dubai dusk somehow seems more sinister now, glistening less like a holiday resort and more like a sewage farm. Someone said they were all here – the Russian mafia, the Chinese mafia, Al-Qaeda. It's the money laundering capital of the Middle East, like Switzerland during the war with spicier food and less snow. (Although apparently someone's building a ski-slope in the middle of a shopping mall.)

Just then my phone rings.

'Jerome where are you? The gig starts in 10 minutes!'

'Long story, see you in a minute.'

Whatever I do it has to be assured. I have a quick whiz round and pick up a couple of empty glasses, put them on a tray with a bottle of Jack Daniel's and head towards the lift. Never has a lift taken so long for its doors to shut. Just outside my field of vision I can feel someone wondering whether to get in or not. In the end they decide to wait for the next one.

It's tempting to mention what I've just seen, from the stage, but that might just get the whole show shut down once and for all. Besides I've just stolen some whisky from some blokes with guns. I've also just spent a few minutes in a confined space with several prostitutes, and now we're all selling our souls for cash.

Prison 𝍷𝍷𝍷𝍷 𝍷𝍷𝍷𝍷 𝍷

It's just a job. Huh, I remember when I used to call it a career.

My stomach groans, like the single note of a cello in a cathedral. I suppose at least this is another 'experience'. But it's not a good experience is it? But maybe there's some material to be had out of it . . .

'You know what it's like when you're in prison in China . . . and then you make a racist remark . . . oh yes, I can hear some laughs of recognition. We've all been there.'

This is going to end up fine. It has to. The life of a stand-up is not an ordinary one. Living on the edge, you have to expect things to go wrong occasionally. Wouldn't change it for the world, though. Well apart from this bit obviously. And some other bits. But not some others though.

Hotel Patrons Only

June 1998: Walk from car to hotel then back again

A car park full of Jags (sleek and vicious), and a handful of BMWs crouch on the gravel like huge toads. There are a few Ferraris too, small and flat, which if they were stones would be really good for skimming. Behind, the hiss of distant traffic seeps across the hedgerows from the M6. In the foreground there are tiny 'clicks' and 'tings' from beneath the shiny bonnets, as the metal cools and contracts.

They're all lined up in the parking overflow at Chimley Manor in Staffordshire, an up-market country hotel that specialises in business conferences. I've just parked my battered VW Golf (belligerently ugly) facing forward for a quick getaway. Appropriately, by comparison it looks like a clown's car (two parps and the doors fall off). It's certainly the only one with child seats lashed into the back. I'm here for a corporate – a gig to some fat cats after dinner.

I open the car door to get out. The air is fresh, and in the distance a pheasant makes a noise like a party blower thing from a Christmas cracker.

Into the foyer, which is all antiques, gold fittings and there's a large open fire. There is a woman in a black trouser suit with her back to me. She's on her mobile.

'. . . no I'm stuck here until the ruddy comedian arrives.'

As she turns round I offer my hand.

'Hello, I'm the ruddy comedian.'

She smiles with her teeth but not her eyes.

'Wendy Appleyard, Production Manager.'

It seems she's suspicious of my profession. She looks at me as if to say 'You will be funny won't you?'. Then she says 'You will be funny won't you?'

'I'll do my best.'

Perhaps she's had a bad experience with a comic, although intermediaries are often dubious of the 'turn' probably because they've worked out our pound per minute ratio compared to theirs.

Yes, this pays well, but it's daunting: 55 middle-aged business-men from a pharmaceutical company. Three Japanese, two Sri Lankans and an American, none of whom speak English. No swearing, speaking to the chairman or mentioning a certain legal case in South Africa which they seem to think I know about. Thirty to forty minutes depending how it's going. (Twenty will be an achievement.)

The big boys – Freddie McKay, Spinola and Co – can charge five figure sums, with an extra few grand added on if they agree to stay and have a drink with the client. But you never know with these gigs, that's why they pay extra, they might just forget to provide you with a microphone, or an audience that wants to listen. In the stress of the moment, as you struggle to find a rhythm you find yourself going back to your oldest jokes, like a confused gadget reverting to factory settings. If you don't concentrate you can take a nose-dive – like when you're coming downstairs and just for a second you just forget how to put one foot in front of the other.

Occasionally your duties can include presenting awards. So you press Perspex plinths into sweaty palms and smile politely as thanks goes to all those without whom it wouldn't have been possible to win Rawlplug of the Year. The worst part is being expected to attend the dinner as well. A rabbit making small talk with ferrets before becoming the entertainment.

We sneak a look at the Constable Suite where it's all happening. It's set out with five large round tables spaced across a huge room with a high ceiling and chandeliers. There are also a couple of pillars in the room obscuring sight-lines. There *is* a microphone, but it's on a small stage in front of an empty dance floor. This means I'll be a good 20 yards from the nearest other person in the room. There's no atmosphere, conversation is just a murmur, and the main sounds are coughing and cutlery.

'Should be fine shouldn't it?' says Wendy still suspicious.

Oh dear, Wendy, stand by for another bad experience with a comedian, not that it will be his fault.

It seems they do these events a lot and there's a whiff of complacency in the air. Drug companies are doing very well thank you. Two hours to wait, before almost certain death. It's best not to stay over – you only get to meet them all again at breakfast. Besides it's a lot quicker to get home at night. But I'm not the only entertainment. Apparently, after me there are some special surprise guests. It's them who're in for a surprise though.

'Don't forget to mention Kerry's shoes!'

Suddenly there's a man with a red face and curly hair looking boggle eyed at me.

'You're the turn aren't you?' he checks.

'Yup' I concede, although it's him who looks more like a clown.

'Don't forget to mention Kerry's shoes!!'

'Right.'

Then he's off nudging people and checking everyone's got a drink.

But who's Kerry? And why are his shoes funny? What is Zippo thinking? It's good to have inside information but you have to be sure of it, otherwise you might trip up and never recover. It's good to think of something bespoke if you can, but even if it goes well, afterwards you'll only have to park it in your unusable joke museum alongside other redundant classics – 'It's nice to be here at the Welsh Grocers' Association, but if you're going to heckle, can I ask you to take a ticket and wait till I call your number' etc.

An hour later I've skimmed all the day's newspapers in the

lounge, which are attached to long wooden rods to stop you walking off with them. In future they might think to do that with acts who've had a look at the room – stick a rod horizontally across their shoulders to stop them running out the door.

Suspicious Wendy comes in to say that they are now onto the main course.

'Nothing to eat?'

'No thanks.'

How do condemned prisoners enjoy a last meal when they're about to face the gallows?

'Well I hope you're better than the one we had last year.'

Ah, now the truth comes out.

'Who was that?'

'Ted . . . Bundle? 'Er . . . Ted Bundass?'

'Tony Tundass?'

'That's him. He arrived late, got drunk and then insulted some of the Nigerian delegates.'

'Ah . . . well that's his speciality. So how come you went for comedy again?'

'There's a new MD. He's a fan of yours. He's seen you at the Comedy Lounge, apparently.'

Great. Just great. They often assume you'll be able to bring with you both your act, and the atmosphere of 400 people crammed into the cellar where they first saw you, into their sparsely populated cathedral of embarrassment.

10.35: 'They're having coffee.'

10.55: 'They're onto the awards.'

She'll be back in a minute, with a priest ideally.

11.10: Suddenly Wendy is not so suspicious.

'I'm really sorry Jerome . . . I hope you don't mind . . . I wouldn't normally ask this . . .'

Oh no they want me to do an hour.

'. . . do you mind if we cancel you?'

'What!?'

'. . . on full pay obviously.'

Trying hard not to laugh out loud, or hug her, I pause for a second, replaying the tape in my head just to check. Yes, 'suddenly conciliatory' Wendy has just asked if I wouldn't mind not facing the firing squad after all.

'Sure, whatever you think best for the night' I mutter, mustering up as much sobriety as possible.

'It's just we're running way behind, and we've got to get the Three Degrees on stage as quickly as possible.'

'Sure . . . sure, the Three Degrees?'

'Yes, they've been flown over specially.'

There's not a moment to lose, in case they change their minds.

'The MD wants to apologise to you himself.'

'No need.'

I'm out the door in a flash.

In the car park I sneak a look through the window of the dining room. The Three Degrees are on stage already and belting out 'When will I see you again?'.

'Anytime' I think to myself. I'd be happy to do gigs like this one every night of the week, lots of them all in different parts of the country at the same time, as long as I don't have to actually turn up, of course.

Now the audience are being told off for not getting on the dance floor. One of the Degrees is having a real go at them – the third one presumably. In the lights the ageing divas don't realise that their audience are almost all men! It's all fascinatingly awkward. I wouldn't like to be in Kerry's shoes!

The air is fresh and I can smell grass cuttings somewhere. The wings of an owl rustle overhead but when it squawks it's already far away. A hunting machine, in and out before anyone knows it. Owls, the SAS and me. A security light comes on as I crunch across the gravel, like an escaped prisoner. Now, which one of these cars is mine?

Prison IHT IHT II

A clown for adults – not even part of the real world. But this is the real world isn't it? I am a martyr for freedom of speech. And the freedom to pull racist faces – in an ironic way obviously, not in a BNP way at all.

The door scrapes open again. There's someone else with them this time. He's thrown in to the cell and cries out as he falls against the metal bunks. He springs back up to pound the door, but stops short when he sees me. Ah. The cell is barely big enough for one. He looks away and finishes a conversation with himself in Chinese. He's lean with sunken cheeks like Bruce Lee, but with even more pockmarks. From the scowl he's giving me, it doesn't look like he's up for collaborating on a sitcom. He's angry, but clearly rattled by my presence. I try not to meet his eye.

Er, are all Chinese good at martial arts? Perhaps they've put a maniac in the same cell to teach me a lesson – Crouching Tiger Hidden Body. He ignores me. What's that noise in the distance? – like an engine pounding on and off? It's my heart!

Twenty minutes later we still haven't spoken, but I've calmed down a little. Pointing at myself I say, 'Jerome'.

His eyes widen at the suddenness of my voice and then he just stares at me. Now I point at him. He throws back an aggressive sound. Was that his name or did he just tell me where to go? Now what do I do?

Another 40 minutes pass. There's no way of knowing who he is or what he's done, if he's guilty or innocent, common thief or political prisoner. My money's on drunken hothead. Suddenly my visitor stands up and pulls a bucket from beneath the bed and uses it. He's been here before. Perhaps he's just been arrested, or moved from another cell and the guards are now betting on our celebrity death-match. Bruce Leak versus Offensive Racial Stereotype man. But what hope is there of explaining who I am or how I got to be here?

Maybe he's a spook, an agent sent to watch me or to obtain a confession. Yes, perhaps he works for Telestar!? They were expanding in the Far East! Perhaps Gary Bidulph's put them up to this to teach me a lesson? Last time I saw him he definitely had revenge on his mind.

Marvellous, just marvellous. Did this really start with me and my sister making silly noises on our tape recorders? Now I wish I could press the rewind button – fast.

Just then my stomach makes an involuntary spurting noise. Like I'm getting a fax. No, the sudden start of a Jean Michel Jarre track – only internal. Another gurgle, lower down. Oh no, not here, not now!

Stay Clear Of The Doors

November 1998: Car back home from
South East London

I'm trying to manoeuvre my way out of the car park onto the grubby South Circular.

I've been doing more benefits than normal recently. Subconsciously, perhaps, trying to balance my karma overdraft, in the hope that somehow it will help Suzy. But like old people who suddenly start feeding the birds it's probably all a bit late. Apparently the latest treatment's not working, so far, anyway. Can't imagine what it's like: in the middle of the night, alone with your tumors.

There's a charity show at a big football club and many of the players are in the audience. You can tell who they are by their body language alone. They seem to look at the stage as if to say 'I'm good at what I do, let's see if you're good at what you do'. Lot's of pretty girls hanging about too.

It was never going to be straightforward. One-off shows rarely are. This is a mish mash of comics, bands and an auction. Someone could come unstuck, but I'm determined it's not going to be me.

I precede a tribute band to the Doors who catch the worst of it.

After stand-up, music seems like an excuse to talk and walk around, or maybe the Doors were just before most people's time. Anyway, in the dressing room afterwards the band blank me as if somehow it's my fault. One of the footballers – no one I'd heard of – has bought me a pint of whisky. But I've decided to leave, and give the glass to the Jim Morrison of the group who brings himself to mutter 'Thanks mate'.

Just then the promoter takes me aside and asks me to go on stage again to get the crowd back after the interval. It's not an appealing prospect. Tonight they have a short attention span, distracted by celebrities. But I sigh and agree, do an encore and leave.

Now there's a flash sports car in front of me blocking the gate. At first he looks like he's going to reverse into the space beside him, but he waits too long. Impatiently I overtake, pulling out quickly, but at the exact same moment the driver reverses, swinging the front end round, clipping my passenger door on the way past. The collision sounds worse than it is. I leap out, and the plastic trim from my door is hanging off.

'You bloody . . . !' I start as if it was a noun, but then just as quickly I run out of steam.

'How dare you!' shrieks a tanned blonde woman getting out the driver's door.

Then the passenger door opens.

'Jerome Stevens!' says Gary Bidulph.

I haven't seen him for a while. He's a big shot now.

'Gary! Do somefing! He's gorn an smashed into us.'

(Is she doing a funny voice?) I don't have the patience for this tonight.

'Oh shut up! You crashed into me! Why don't we call the police?'

After this flash of temper a different look crosses Gary's face.

'Listen Jerome, if you call the police, my girlfriend and I will tell them that you overtook on the wrong side of the road without indicating, and that you were speeding.'

'. . . You'd lie then?'

He shrugs.

'Of course you would, you're an agent. You're Mickey Spinola's agent for goodness sake.'

'Bit-ter' scoffs Gary.

Then turning to the woman I surprise myself with a slightly sinister tone. 'You realise the consequences of this for your relationship don't you?' (Now this is dangerous territory: not only have I lost my temper, but now I'm also about to employ work skills, without the back up of any kind of security.)

'What d'ya mean?' she says a little frightened.

'If he's prepared to lie at the drop of a hat . . . you'll never be able to trust him again will you? You've just seen how quickly he's prepared to try to cover his tracks.'

'Wha' she ponders.

There's a bit of quiet. Their car engine is still running. Gary eyeballs me for a second, as if to say 'you haven't heard the last of this'. Then he gets into his car and slams the door. The woman gives me a glance, then gets in beside him. Was that awe or disgust? I'm not quite sure. Hurriedly they start up and lurch forward into the gloom. Someone claps. It's the one of the Doors I gave the whisky to, who's having a smoke outside. Instinctively I acknowledge the applause.

Well well, normally even comedians think of what they should have said on the way home. But I'm not usually that angry. The Suzy thing is definitely affecting me more than I realise.

Pull

As we buckle up, I seem to remember people lying half naked in the gutter groaning, but I've only had two hours' sleep and now the images of last night, like a shabby box of receipts, all need sorting into chronological order.

I wonder if they have retirement homes for old stewardesses, and if when they're about to take-off for their final destination in the sky, all their relatives file past so that they can say 'Goodbye, bye, bye, bye bye, bye, bye . . .'

Three shows in casinos in Ibiza. A sunny outpost of Essex in the Balearics. Hotels with balconies covered in union jacks and whole bars dedicated to television programmes like *EastEnders* and *Only Fools and Horses*. (None to *Panorama* or *University Challenge*, I notice.)

I left Marita with a birthday party to clear up. Stan was seven, a few days ago and twelve of his friends had trashed the place for three long hours. Perhaps we shouldn't have called it a 'Wild party'. To make it worse I'd forgotten to tell Marita I was escaping to Spain that evening. All that, and we're pregnant again. I think we're going to have to move house this time. Well, I am.

The captain comes on. A Captain? I wonder if he could be court-martialled for abusing passengers, like soldiers in the Gulf – for taking pictures of himself smiling, beside a tall man sitting in economy. No one's listening. But part of me feels like I should be a good audience. A stewardess tells us what to do if we come down on land or in the water, but exploding in mid-air seems to be glossed over. 'Put both arms out at right angles and flap up and down like this . . .'

The shows are simple enough, and by that I mean we have to keep them simple. Obvious stuff, pull faces and pick on people. But at least they're up for it, and they are still up for it afterwards as well. Normally I go home after a show, but no chance of that here. Besides, there's something about the sweaty agoraphobia of performing that makes you crave the warmth of human affirmation (difficult to explain to a partner who can only see that you seem to have had a lot of attention already). But there are times when we want to be able to step off the stage and be welcomed back into the bosom of mankind, or if you're Eric Bowman, preferably the bosoms of womankind.

They show us round every bar in town. I'm with Bowman and Danny Bullen and we're all keen to please our mobile audience. Everyone wants to meet the comedians. We're in a bar some-where. The music is the sort of Belgian techno pop that you only tolerate on holiday, the type that sounds as if there's a demented squirrel in the background crashing two bin lids together. Then there's another round of shots, guava flavour as I recall.

Occasionally you hear of someone who survives falling out of a plane without a parachute. Falls into a snowdrift or onto a bouncy castle. Presumably for every one of those there's another, who lands just beside a bouncy castle or onto some railings. That would be me.

Bowman is a predator. He can sniff out consent over hundreds of metres, even if there are only a few parts per million; and he's surprisingly successful, given that he looks like a history teacher. In reality I think he's so calloused he doesn't notice the knock-backs. Now he's sitting with a teenage girl on each knee and another one is feeding him a kebab. Classy. But there's something about this picture that is eerily familiar – Bowman is a ventriloquist.

'I see Eric's trying out some new dummies' I say to Danny.

He replies deadpan 'Yeah, they need to watch where his hands go.'

Maybe I'm just jealous. We'd all like to know if we could, if we wanted to.

Some people are afraid of flying. But when you think about the facts *everyone* should be afraid of flying. Tiny petrol-filled darts criss-crossing the skies at hundreds of miles an hour.

Just then there are raised voices. Someone's pushing someone. A scream. The muscle-bound boyfriend of one of the girls has turned up. He surges at Eric pointing a finger. The music stops, the rest of the crowd groan. Some of them surround Eric to protect him, a bottle is thrown.

You know where you are with a saloon fight in a Western. Cowboys take it in turn to crack each other on the chin until there's one man left standing, he'll wipe a trickle of blood from his mouth, finish his drink and stumble through the flappy doors and out into the street. In a real brawl the fighting is less choreographed. Most of the punches don't seem to land at all, and when they do there is just a muffled thud. When a chair gets brought down on someone's head it doesn't automatically smash into hundreds of pieces, in this case it just makes a 'kwok' sound as the side of a cheek caves in. Someone on the floor doesn't necessarily play dead until he grabs the leg of his opponent sending him flying across the room. Here he lies sobbing 'please stop, please stop' as his assailant continues to kick him, deliberately aiming for the kidneys.

Danny and I are frozen to the spot – not even ducking behind the bar, or trying to play the piano. There are just two or three staggering about now, one has blood pouring out of his sandal, he must have stood on some glass – no one really does that in a movie either. Eric, however, is nowhere to be seen. Just then several Spanish policemen with truncheons arrive, apparently disappointed to have missed the action. They stop a couple of lads trying to crawl away through the detritus. Danny and I quickly make our way behind the bar and out the back.

'What happened to Eric?' I wonder.

'I thought he took a hit.'

'We should go back.'

'We might get arrested, you know what foreign police are like.'

Danny's right. We watch from a distance as five or six Brits are thrown in the back of Policia vans, some of whom weren't even fighting. Within minutes the floor is being swept, the music is back on and new punters are coming into the club. I don't know where the people with injuries went. We escaped, that's all that seems to matter.

A sudden roar. A burst of speed. Try to look nonchalant. My palms are sweating. I have a headache. How can hundreds of tons of metal swoop into the air when I literally can't even fly a kite? The overhead storage lockers creak as we climb. Beside me Danny is hidden behind a sleeping mask like a snoozing Zorro. Now we are high enough to see several different towns, each one looking disconcertingly like the site of an ancient plane crash, debris strewn over a large area. We head into a cloud. And out again. Up here the clouds aren't cloud shaped, they're weird coral accretions like chimneys, while others are like giant padded furniture, misty cream sofas and inflated gothic wardrobes. Back in again. And out once more into the kingdom of mashed potato, and the gloriously hot butter of the yellow sun. I must be hungry. I wonder if we get anything to eat?

Danny and I make our way to another bar and order two coffees.

'We'll see if he turns up at the hotel later.'

'He'd better, our flight's first thing in the morning.'

Someone starts up the jukebox.

'Not that song again.'

'Look!'

'What? That girl with the hair?

'No, look who she's dancing with!'

'Bowman!'

It must be some sort of illness.

Keep Your Distance

Dawn is breaking and my stomach is turning over with a mixture of excitement, guilt and strawberries. We stop at traffic lights on the Cromwell Road. Each round light is made up of lots of thin lines of neon. Giant electric fruit gums they are. I thought a red light meant 'Stop', but apparently not if you're a cyclist. Yes, the Bike People are beginning to evolve separately now, making up their own rules and wearing alien helmets.

What's My Lie? is a pilot for a new panel game on a cable channel.
   'It's a real honour to be asked' gushes Gordon my agent.
   'Syd Little's dropped out.'
   We pitch up mid morning and have everything explained to us over coffee. There are two teams of two – a comedian and a star from the world of entertainment on each side. Pete Pendleton and Colin Whittard – the retired 400 metre hurdler – are facing me, and former eighties pop siren, Zafira. This is a special thrill for me, for if there was one person who represented glamour and unattainable beauty to me as a teenager, it was Zafira. I bought two of her albums and made Suzy put up the posters that came with them. I also recall her from the seventies kids' TV programme *Billy's Wheels*. She's delighted that someone remembers the show and we hit it off straight away.

We go through the structure of the rounds with the producer, but there are several moments I catch myself just staring open-mouthed thinking 'You're Zafira!' At one point I almost phone Ralph, to have her talk to him on my mobile, but he can be a bit abrupt with strangers, and I decide against it after imagining him saying something like 'What, are you still alive?'

I've done a couple of panel games before. If you're on with some chatterboxes you can all too easily seize up, as if standing at a crowded urinal. On a historical quiz for radio a few years ago I think the longest sentence I managed was 'Goodbye everyone!'.

In the late afternoon we go through the actual questions we're going to get that evening. (Yes it's all worked out beforehand, although you wouldn't necessarily know it.) The writers riff and busk ideas, jumping from one to the next like noisy insects – talking and eating biscuits all at once. I think they must have been the clever but excitable children at school, the ones who were no good at sport, stayed in at break and laughed a bit too much at bodily functions. But they're not as vain as stand-ups, they can't afford to be – their ideas are kicked around and easily shelved, and if one gets through to the actual show, it could easily get murdered in the delivery by a semi-famous chef or sportsman. I've learnt to save my best thoughts for the night itself, because sharing them too early may tempt someone into blurting them out before you do. Just test out the ones you're not sure about beforehand.

Zafira seems to find it all a little tiresome, and several times I fetch her water. But at about half five we're all sent into make-up and the producer gives us a pep talk, before announcing that he's going to go and have a look at the audience.

'Is there a live audience!?' starts Colin Whittard.

'Of course' says the producer taken back.

This is obviously a hurdle Colin wasn't expecting, and he suddenly becomes very nervous and calls his agent. Zafira on the other hand, who doesn't seem to have paid any attention all day, on the night, sparkles brilliantly.

Usually I despise the contrivance and fake bonhomie of such

shows, because usually beneath the thinly disguised smiles is a desperate raw competitiveness. Not to win the game, of course, but just to beat anyone else to saying something funny. But tonight there's something about being asked lots of questions you've only half prepared, that makes me jump in the deep end, and I carry it off with something approaching style. Zafira and I actually enjoy ourselves, sparking off each other like an old married couple.

The cab takes no time at this hour. It's unlicensed, the sort you're probably not supposed to use, driven by a man of Mediterranean appearance (olive not blue). He drives very fast setting off several speed cameras.

There are drinks after the show. Everyone is very pleased, except true to form Colin has done a runner. After a couple of hours the party has thinned out and Zafira invites us all back to hers. I should go home – but it's Zafira! How often do you get the chance to go to her place? Besides Marita won't be up and we haven't exactly been getting on lately. She works days, I work nights. There's an overlap, but we always seem to be chaperoned by the evil pixies that live with us. Too much to do and no quality time – ships that pass in the early evening.

It's a large four-storey house off Sloane Square. We seem to lose a few more of the party on the way, but there are some rock music types already hanging about at her place. Magically two enormous bowls of strawberries appear which is just what everyone feels like on a hot summer's night.

I spend a couple of hours bluffing my way through a conversation about world music to a huge Cuban bass player with dreadlocks, who Zafira met while recording in South America. He gets to hear me jam my top three comedy anecdotes. Then I catch up with Lennie Parks who has dropped in on his way back from the airport after a tour of New Zealand. We get on to Mickey Spinola, Lennie has had gags lifted too, but he just shrugs his shoulders.

'It's a shame for people like Jack Patrick, he's had almost his whole act swiped and now he's in rehab. But for you and me mate . . . perhaps we should just be glad that our gags are out there – giving people pleasure.'

I have no answer to this. But I tell him about crashing into Bidulph's car, and he laughs and says 'They've lost their soul, man. You don't want to let those people wind you up. They've lost their soul.'

Champagne and reefers come and go and then through one of the Georgian windows I catch a glimpse of dawn breaking. The sky is red. Isn't that some sort of warning?

Home. This is where I live. The cab makes a racket in the silent street. I pay the driver with notes and tell him to keep the change – coins make too much noise. He turns round in one arc, then rattles off towards town and into the day ahead. One bird is singing in the birch tree opposite. Pure lucid notes that seem to be asking a question – and whatever it is the answer's 'no comment'.

'Shut up will you! What are you trying to do, wake everyone up?'

That's exactly what he's trying to do of course. This is the beginning of the dawn chorus. The gate creaks, and then I scrunch a snail on the path. Spiders have left gossamer threads to try and garrotte their victim – the whole of nature has turned against me. The key in the lock makes the noise of opening up Alcatraz and for a moment I'm trapped in someone else's tiresome routine about coming in drunk from the pub. Now the floorboards! What, am I walking on the keys of a piano? My stomach feels bitter.

Back at the party my watch had said half five and I thought I should make a move. I nipped upstairs to get my coat, but I couldn't remember which room . . . . I try a door but there's someone under the covers who stirs as the light comes on.

'S-sorry.'

It's Zafira! Her big eyes open and she smiles as she stretches out against the satin sheets. Her arms are bare, and for a second the pose reminds me of one of her album covers. I stare too long.

'Er, just looking for my coat . . . thought I'd better go.'

Then she looks away with a twinkle of mischief.

'You don't have to go if you don't want to . . .'

No Swimming

August 1999: Doggy paddle
in the shallow end

'Not so funny now are you?'

I stand up, suddenly confronted with the same group of lads that sat in the front row last night. Except now we are all naked. Well as good as, face to face in the municipal swimming pool.

'I – I'm here with my son' I stutter defensively, trying to justify my presence in the beginners' pool, and then I pull Stan close, using him as a human shield. This is supposed to be 'man time' with my boy– learning to swim and taking the splashes of life in the eye. But it's only been 10 minutes and now I'm freezing and want to go home.

My old adversaries stand silhouetted against the morning sun by the side of the pool. It's like the Sheriff of Nottingham's men happening upon Robin Hood as he bathes in a brook. I gave them quite a hard time, you see – they were all trainee estate agents whom, I suggested, would only be getting one and a half per cent of the jokes. But to be fair they were the ones who laughed the most. Yes, I'd also found a solicitor in the room and asked her how she'd like it if I left six months between set up and punch line. It proved a popular attack on the night; I just wasn't expecting to meet any of them again so soon.

Sometimes you get flashbacks to the night before, or the night before the night before and you re-live the moment in the cold light of day and think 'Did I really say that?' Or 'Here's what I should have said'. But this morning I'm the flashback, and now it looks as if the people I picked on will get the chance to wreak their revenge without me being able to hide behind a microphone, rehearsed put-downs or clothes even.

Were all swimming baths built in the sixties? They all seem to be grey and square, which makes them feel colder somehow. As we came in I'd spun sideways towards a drinks machine on thinking that I saw that bloke Alfie coming out of the changing rooms. Stan couldn't believe his luck – hot chocolate before swimming as well! But it wasn't my loyal fan; it was just someone with the same shape and sound. I felt both relieved and strangely disloyal.

'So where are you all from?' I say automatically.

'You asked us that last night' says the longhaired leader.

'Oh yes, Wimbledon wasn't it. Nice one.'

I pause for a second, instinctively making the link between estate agents, sharks and swimming, but it seems a bit desperate and I'm feeling vulnerable, so I drop it. But the onus is definitely on me to drive the conversation, given that I'm 'the funny one'.

'I hate swimming. My son loves it. Once you get to a certain age, it's just getting wet and cold really.'

No laughs there, they haven't got to that age yet. After all, they're here voluntarily.

'We let him see the film *Titanic* the other day, thought some bits might scare him, but he loved the boat going down, it was the snogging he couldn't stand.'

This gets a laugh, although I think it's mainly the word 'snogging' that does it. But now Stan is just staring, terrified by the strange boy-men his Daddy is talking to.

'I think your Speedos are scaring the kid, Chris' says one of them, and they all laugh again, turning sideways, pushing each other, and grinning. Yes, all the others apart from Chris are in

Bermuda shorts. He blushes. Even the top of his chest goes red. I just grin like a hapless supply teacher.

A whistle! It comes from a bored lifeguard slouched on a stool up a small ladder. Now he's pointing at some kids who were running along the side. I wonder if his Mum spotted his potential at an early age as he sat in his high chair?

Then one of the gawky outlines scratches his face self-consciously and takes a genuine tone. 'Must be a hard job though, being a comedian.'

They all agree.

'Sometimes, yeah sometimes.'

(This catches me off guard. Should have got off on *Titanic*, moved away, said we had to go – this is probably why TV stars have their own swimming pools.)

'Well I couldn't do what you do' says Chris.

They all shake their heads.

Another kid jumps in nearby and I flinch pathetically. Stan wants to be lifted and I feign annoyance at the bomber on his behalf. But I'm grateful for the warmth of his little torso, as he garlands my neck with his rubbery limbs. We've been stood about for too long now, we're getting really cold, and all my fingers and toes have developed tiny pads the texture of walnuts.

'Oh, you get used to it' I offer.

None of us are too sure what to do now.

'Chris was in the Olympics!' says one of them.

Chris shuffles with more embarrassment.

Why isn't doggy paddle a race in the Olympics? It's a ridiculous stroke, scrabbling about like a squirrel burying a nut, head proud like a sphinx. Yes, the four thousand-metre doggy paddle, with clothes pegs on their noses – I'd pay to watch that.

'Seriously?' I say catching up.

'No, Commonwealth Games' says Chris.

'Yeah, diving – he's well good.'

'Show him Chris!'

'Yeah go on Chris' they all join in.

Chris is literally pushed into performing – I know how he feels. But once he gets to the other end of the baths and the diving pool, he fearlessly strides up the three flights of steps to the top board, as if he's just nipping upstairs to fetch a can of Lynx.

He halts for a second, up near the ceiling, feet well over the edge. All the echoey shouts and splashes stop for a second, as everyone turns to watch. Then in an instant, he twists and somersaults several times and enters the water with a tiny 'plip!'. Spontaneous applause from friends and strangers alike. Wow Chris, I couldn't do what you do either.

Beware Children

A huge explosion.
'That's it Dad.'
'What!?'

It's six o'clock in the morning and apparently I've just lost another game of *Star Wars* pod racer on the Nintendo. It wouldn't be so bad, but this time Reg has beaten me using only his feet. At least now I can go to bed. Dawn is . . . dawning again, I'm beginning to dream while standing up, and my skin against my clothes feels like the inside of a greased cake tin.

Although it only finished six and a half hours ago the freshers' gig at Keele University feels like it was sometime last year. Can't do much more of this. Last night I had the realisation that the whole audience was born while I was at college, and the other day when drying my hair there was a vein on my head I'd never seen before.

But I'd promised to give the little chap a game two days ago, before forgetting and going up North. I'm determined to be a good Dad, determined not to look back on this time and regret pushing my children away. Promise kept then.

Marita is still asleep. Must wash. Discard clothing. Stumble into the shower knocking showerhead out of the holder. Clatters to the floor. Keep finding grey hairs – see them everywhere. In my hair, in my sons' hair, recently even felt a tinge of sadness for a porcupine we saw at a petting zoo, because the tips of its quills were white. It was the one we visited when I was playing the Devizes Festival. Oh yes – as we set off as a family in the morning, we gave a cheery wave to the stragglers who were coming into the hotel foyer from the night before. This must be how they felt. The worst thing about feeling old is a growing sense that you've had your go, that the music has started again and you've had to pass the parcel on. (A porcupine in a petting zoo?)

I remember when the bar at Keele University was named after Nelson Mandela. These days it's called something like Vibe 21. In my day students were angry and went on demonstrations, now they're too busy paying their grants back. (Did I just say 'in my day'?)

I noticed on the motorway last night that the cars of this generation seem to be all the same, with large glass headlamps and similar curves, lacking in character. Being a comedian is now a mainstream career choice, a module of English or Drama at certain universities. Yes, now there are all sorts of courses and competitions to help you get on, find a voice, pretend to be angry about something. Humbug. But at least there's more money in it now.

Now I'm brushing my teeth.
  'BOH!'
  'Hello Stan.'
  'BOH!'
  'What?'
  'It's my new word.'
  'What is?'
  'Boh – it's for surprising people, when things are dull.'
  'Well, please don't do it now, I've got a headache.'

Student audiences are usually quite easily led, and last night was like doing a school assembly. These kids haven't experienced enough of life to have their own opinions, and they're more likely to laugh at what they think they should. But you have to be firm, after all it might be the first time they've experienced interactive entertainment that doesn't have a pause button. (At another college gig I know, if they don't like you, they turn on the big TV and watch *Casualty* instead.) As usual, just make an example of the first person to stick their head above the parapet.

These days every phone box is a university and it seems that now you can find 'A' levels at the bottom of cereal packets. This means all sorts are enjoying a college education that, in the past, would have just got a job cutting grass in the park. (That's probably a course now too.)

The other type of student show is where no one pays to get in and they're all just discovering alcohol. (Those are the ones that make you feel really old.)

The gig took a while to get going. Then I had them. Then it really took off. But 20 minutes in, I noticed that they weren't quite laughing in the right places. Then I looked down and saw the red dot of a laser pen hovering around the top of my trousers. They were happy, but sometimes you have to wonder what the point of it all is. Nights like this weren't in the plan.

Recently we took the kids to a fair where there was a Punch and Judy stall. The old boy had all the traditional gear, complete with original Victorian hand-carved puppets. But entertainment has moved on. Eventually the small crowd dwindled until he was left with three small boys at the front chanting 'boring!, boring!, boring!'.

Of course what would've entertained students 10 years ago probably won't do now. It's not just a case of dropping stuff about Thatcherism and Salad Cream, and replacing it with hilarious insights on global warming and Britney Spears. But the language itself, the ideas and the juxtapositions have to remain unpredictable. Styles of comedy have a sell by date too, and you have to keep up. The circuit moves imperceptibly like a glacier, and if you stay still long enough you will be crushed. Several comics have given up only to come back after a few years to find that a voice that was once dissident, is now mainstream and has lost all its edge.

On the other hand, some comics have said the same words in the same venues so many times that the audience could join in, as if with the Lord's Prayer at a school assembly. Some routines have even been around so long, like Abba and flared trousers, they've passed from 'tired' to 'classic'. The American military, and gun dealers around the world, would probably welcome any second Gulf War, but not half as much as Danny Bullen – whose Desert Storm material will soon be coming up for its 10 year anniversary.

The shower is only lukewarm – of course the hot water won't have come on yet. If I stay in too long it might wake me up. As I dry myself I can see my own breath – the heating isn't on either. I'm desperate to dive under the heavy warm clouds of the duvet.

'Dad's going to bed now' I explain.

'Do you think one day Dad, that men will walk around with suckers on the ceiling?'

If I were a real father I'd use this as an opportunity to talk about gravity or technology or something. But before I get much of a chance to reply more questions come in a barrage.

'Why are my teeth sharp? What happens when you die? Why did you throw a pillow at me? Is it because you're a comedian, Dad? Where do comedians go when they die?'

'Keele University' I reply.

'Why did you laugh Dad?'

More general explosions as he returns to a galaxy far away.

In the bedroom now, and I climb in beside Marita. Cuddle up.

What's this? She's left a note for me. It's a receipt with the word 'Sensations' circled and she's put a big question mark beside it. Sensations? Sensations? That sounds like a make of condom or something. The date is a few months ago. Perhaps I won't sleep quite as well as I thought.

'Dad? Dad?'
'Ssh Mum's asleep.'
'Why are there no female butchers?'
'What!? Female butchers? Aren't there?'
'BOH!'
'Go away!'

Prison ⊞⊞ ⊞⊞ III

Sensations are crisps. I bought them in Sainsbury's last time I was there, two for the price of one. When I find the receipt, I go to the cupboard and throw both packets at Marita as she sits on the sofa. She laughs out loud. I'm relieved.

Not that there was anything to find out – I didn't sleep with Zafira or anyone else. I couldn't. Not after the dreadlocked head of that Cuban bass player suddenly appeared between the sheets as well. I just made my excuses and left. Didn't even get the chance to make a decision – I think that's why I'm feeling guilty. But I'm a loyal person aren't I? Come on, I felt bad phoning up and changing electricity provider. But this would have changed everything. It just didn't feel like a major junction, that's all.

It's seven in the morning now. So it's around midnight at home, they'll all be fast asleep. My cellmate has nodded off too. My stomach seems to have calmed down. After all I haven't eaten anything.

I wonder what photo of me they will use on the News? Passport or that one I used for my Edinburgh poster two years ago, rowing a boat in a cup of tea. I can see it now 'British comedian in hot water . . .'. (The show was called 'Storm in a Teacup', but it sank without trace. With hindsight perhaps the title helped the critics a bit too much.)

Comedians usually look like they're trying too hard in photos. Goggle eyes, zany hair, and a manic grin – not images suited to gaining public sympathy. 'Let them wipe that smile off his face' you can hear them think. Performers' photos are usually out of date and often the freak shot from a roll that makes them seem better looking than they are.

When members of the public die or go missing most relatives seem to be caught by surprise, and have to give the Press a badly cropped school or wedding photo, or even a blurred snap of their loved one at a barbecue. Not the image they'd want to leave the world with – wearing an apron, their eyes half shut, holding out a chop. Everyone should get a just-in-case-of-emergency-photo done, one that actually resembles them, slightly serious, perhaps with a gun to their head – so everyone realises the danger they could be in. Maybe you could get sponsorship, a big Nike tick or something – although 'just do it' is probably not the subliminal message you want to send your captors.

There's a fly! No spider for me – just a fly. Making its way uncertainly towards the bucket in the corner. Stopping and starting. Like a pizza delivery boy on a moped checking house numbers.

Bruce stirs and then leaks into the bucket again. Yes. He's definitely had a lot to drink. I wonder if the fly survived that? It never rains, then it pours.

Suppose I don't come back. If I get shot or beaten to death, will anybody notice? Of course my family will notice, there'll be an empty place at the Christmas table, and no one to grumble at the quality of the gags in the crackers.

But in terms of having 'made a difference' in the world, obviously I haven't scratched the surface, or even wiped it with a damp cloth. I've done a few benefits I suppose. And once someone sent me a note saying it was 'the first time they'd laughed since the baby died'. (Glad I didn't meet them though, wouldn't have known what kind of face to pull.) Then there was that old folks' home I did for a friend before I knew better. They just tutted and snored. (Okay I probably shouldn't have started with 'I'm glad I got on early in case some of you died'.)

Yeah I've put in a few tours of duty. But perhaps soon I'll be like a Coke bubble that reaches the surface, pops, and then goes the wrong way up God's nose.

Also, I can't help feeling that this whole episode will look like what I used to do when I was little – an attempt to drag the attention back to me. When Suzy passed an exam or painted a picture beyond her years, her jealous little brother would often go and smash a window or wee behind the sofa. Sorry Suzy.

No Hand Signals

July 2000: Walk from Waterloo
to Oxford Circus

They should turn the tube into a giant ghost train. I'm not sure I can suffer its hot air and banging about this afternoon, I'll walk from here. I need a breath of air. Turn my phone off. Recently I've been so busy that the only place I can relax is actually on stage. It's as if I'm followed everywhere by a swarm of wasps – annoying, making demands and all trying to sting me for time and attention.

Still this is what I wanted isn't it? But it's difficult to switch off, even so-called 'quality time' with the kids seems to have become just an opportunity to read stories with silly voices and improvise with coloured plastic props. Then I'm supposed to be looking for somewhere else to live as well. I long for a night off. But any spare time has to be spent writing, keeping just ahead of my own band wagon, not daring to stop in case it runs me over. Hours and hours are spent sitting in front of a computer screen like a physicist, playing with formulae and balancing equations. Plotting mental firework displays to ambush the punters.

The huge Victorian station echoes with announcements. Passengers decant from long metal worms that come and go under the huge vaulted ceiling, like ants picking clean a whale carcass. There's the Eurostar! A snake with a duck's bill. In a couple of hours I could be in Paris or Brussels or the *real* Waterloo. I could start a new life in Lille or Antwerp. With a girl called Lilley and a boy called Anthony, who is a twerp. (Sometimes I wish I could turn my head off.)

Down the steps, past the taxis, coffee shops and beggars. On to the footbridge across the Thames. I feel more at home in London now. Well, I work in the city.

My programme on Radio Four was only a few minutes away from the bongs of Big Ben, after all. A series would be nice. We did a pilot last month and it was put out at 11.00pm last Thursday, and now we're waiting to hear about doing some more. I'm off to see Harry, the producer, at Broadcasting House to discuss what we'd do if they say 'yes'.

It took ages to get on, and communicating with the BBC feels like dealing with the KGB. Creaking bureaucracy and reels of red tape, but some incredible specialists locked away in the bunker. For our show I'd written a sketch about what would happen if a mole, a rat and a toad actually did go on a boat trip together, as in *The Wind in the Willows* – ie it would be a great big fight. Tentatively I'd asked if there were any suitable sound effects. After a few hours they got back to say they'd found three suitable animal fights, and did I want more aggression from the toad or the rat?

The London Eye: I wish it would go round really fast!

It's been a good discipline. Stand-ups tend to take the line of least resistance, writing and performing simply what works, with no outside interference. Working in a different medium stretches your capabilities. We recorded the pilot in front of an audience of tourists and pensioners at the BBC theatre. Nice of them to come, but I got the impression they all came to a lot of recordings and indeed some of them had even brought sandwiches.

On radio you can't cheat by pulling faces or playing the crowd, it's all words, obviously. But at least, because it is only words, you can just stand there and read it from the script. And because it's recorded you can do re-takes at the end, which, strangely, the audience seem to enjoy more than the actual show.

The money's pretty poor, in fact hour for hour I'm sure I'd have earned more by temping. But then you are standing in the place where all the old greats started out. Already I'm turning my thoughts to telly – can't enjoy the moment. And if and when I'm on TV, no doubt my thoughts will then turn to films, and then ruling the world, other planets and so on.

Suzy turned up to the show in a hat. Halfway through the recording I suddenly realised why – her hair must have started falling out. She avoided chemotherapy to begin with but now it appears that awful heckler has returned and still means deadly business. Just about kept going. She was strangely radiant in the pub afterwards and enthused about everything.

Trafalgar Square! – the very centre of town. Where New Year is counted in, where demonstrations end up and where 'miles to London' are measured to. A must-see destination for pigeons from around the world – to be photographed standing on the heads of the indigenous tourists. The place is dwarfed of course, by Nelson's Column, a life-like statue of a national hero very high in the sky – perhaps there was a mix up with the builders over yards and inches.

Although it was only one programme, I can already feel that I'm touching a different audience to the club circuit, and I'm amazed how many people happened to hear it. A neighbour, a Mum from school and Auntie Andrea in Tamworth's been in touch for the first time in ages. (Didn't say what she thought of it though.)

I've also had a couple of rambling technicolour letters from madmen already. The oddest thing was listening to my programme in the car as I came back from a gig, stopping at the lights, realising that the little man with a moustache in the car opposite was listening to it too. I couldn't tell if he was smiling or not, but at least he didn't turn it off. It was then that it dawned on me. I was on the *radio*! A voice in people's cars, living rooms and ultimately in their heads. I could begin to change the world, if I had something to say. Meanwhile we'll have to get by with some silly sketches.

That's the thing; you record these words in a nice little theatre, but have no idea where they will be listened to. I wonder what Louis Armstrong would make of 'What a Wonderful World' being played in the background of the lighting department in Debenhams?

Oxford Street, the type of people found along here haven't changed for centuries – beggars, buskers and hawkers. And I suppose, as I go to a meeting about a possible radio series, I'm a strange combination of all three.

No – I don't want a leaflet about a language school. A tramp lies in a doorway. He could be dead, as a result of drink, drugs or perhaps a leaflet allergy.

I particularly enjoyed the tone of the continuity announcer who came on after our show. There was a pause and then he said 'That was Jerome Stevens . . .', as if he was wearing a dinner jacket and he'd been forced to pick up an old sock with a pair of tongs.

'. . . and now *Today in Parliament*' he hurriedly continued as if now he had to go and wash his hands. There's something about Radio Four that makes you feel as if you're performing in front of your aunts and uncles at Christmas. And that if there are any children listening, they're only allowed to as a treat between playing Scrabble and music lessons, before being sent to their rooms, whose walls are covered with posters of all the old kings and queens of England.

This feels good – striding in to the BBC and introducing myself at the desk as if to say 'you know – me from last Thursday evening before the news, did you catch it?'.

But it appears they didn't, so I have to wait for Harry to come down and sign me in.

Accident

It's all over. It's 3am and I'm holding a parking ticket. But it
doesn't matter. It doesn't matter at all.

It's the fastest 20-minute set of my career. Thirteen, in fact. But
I've had the call – Marita's gone into labour. Sure, I was at the
boys' births, but I didn't have to rush off stage, mainly because
I didn't have so many gigs to go to in those days. It's a 50-minute
drive, 40 tonight.

   I shouldn't have this much energy. Last night I only had four
hours' sleep and three days ago we moved into a new house just
round the corner from our last one. (I saw a TV programme once,
where Social Services were trying to evict an old man who'd
hoarded everything for years and now his house was full of
rubbish and vermin. Yeah, I think we've just bought *that* house.
But apparently it has 'potential'. Possibly in the same way Hitler
had potential as an artist.)

The hospital car park's full. Don't tell me there's a waiting list. No,
here's a space, how much is it? No one's got that much change! If
it's a long labour the cost will be on a par with us going private.
Well, anyone who gives me a ticket tonight will get strangled with
an umbilical cord.

Marita is lying back and bracing herself for contractions that are coming every three minutes. But this time, as I look around I don't see a delivery room, but the scene of a thousand *Punch* cartoons, TV sketches and stand-up routines. Pompous Carry-on doctors, apoplectic mothers and dopey dads moaning about the pain of missing the football etc. Wisely I keep these thoughts to myself, for fear of becoming a character in my own farce. People in gowns wander in, examining, inspecting and offering words of bored encouragement.

'You're three centimetres' says one of them to Marita.

'She's a lot taller than that' I say, to lighten the mood. But it doesn't.

The doctor sympathetically raises an eyebrow at Marita, smiles a perfunctory smile and then swishes out of the room.

'I bet he doesn't even work here!' I chuckle to my wife. Although she looks like she's regretting being married to me now. I've mentally geared myself for a long haul – the other two took ages.

Our family dynamic is about to change forever and we don't know how. Yes, I'm just about to meet a stranger who's going to leap into my top five people of all time. Now you don't see them – then you do! In a few hours I'll be prepared to kill or die for them.

It's quiet here in the car park. Enjoy this bit. When they've all left home I won't be able to wander into their rooms and watch them breathing. Or if I do, they'll call the police. How would it be, I wonder, if they were all born as fully formed adults? Ouch, no poor Marita, that wouldn't work. But what if all expectant parents gathered in an arrivals lounge ready to greet their fully grown children. We could hold a sign up with our surname on it, and then they would come through the gate carrying all their emotional baggage.

Just then Dr Eyebrow is back and he's rustling up everyone else as well. Showtime! That was quick. They dim the lights and off goes the music. I hadn't noticed it before.

Marita screams. I should do something. Say something. I'm holding her hand. I've told her she can squeeze as hard as she likes. Instead I squeeze *her* hand. Well I'm nervous, what if it all goes wrong? They say it's supposed to be one of the happiest days of your life but each stage has too much stress to enjoy. Is the baby all right? Is Marita all right? Is that normal? Are they still all right? And what if . . . – right up until they are teenagers and beyond, presumably.

'Keep going, not much longer' I say, as if she could stop, and I have absolutely no idea how long it will go on either. But this time it *isn't* long. Here we go. It's the colours that surprise me again. The blood and the bile. Blue, red, green, brown. (Is there a snooker joke in there? . . . no.) The mess and the shouting, the tension and then the release. I suppose it's like well, giving birth really, its own ultimate metaphor.

Just then, a tiny independent squawk. Then a breath, and a louder squawk. It's alive! A boy! Another one. Of course it is. None of us will ever be the same again. It is a magical moment. I should know, I've seen a lot of magic. I don't mean card tricks by magicians that just mean they've practised a lot. I mean moments of creative spontaneity that make audiences gasp. A miracle, a something-out-of-nothing-I-was-there-moment. This is one of those. Except this is life-changing, and it's just for us.

Now the parking ticket seems less like an insult, and more like a souvenir. A fly in the ointment. But the fly is so small compared to the massive tub of ointment, oh yes, and we'll need one of those again – there'll be nappies to be changed!

The team have left us, and Marita is lying back exhausted and I'm holding a tiny warm dead weight in the crevice of my arm. He's small and helpless, yet once again it's me who feels vulnerable.

Life has burst out once more. It's going to get messy and surprising and hypnotising and exhausting all over again. And then there will also be that extra drip, drip of worry about them wherever they are, like the faint knowledge of an appliance left on, the feeling of a limb outside the tent.

'Hello Mister' I say eventually.

He stares back indignantly. Another tough crowd.

Prison ЖН ЖН IIII

_____

I wonder, will Arthur instinctively wake up, knowing his Dad is in danger? According to Mum who was babysitting, both Reg and Stan woke up crying at what must have been the exact moment he was born (wasting no time in competing for attention).

There are tracks on his arm! He's a junkie. Just then I catch his eye. He stares back defiantly. 'So you chase the dragon, no no I hope you really catch him' I try and say with just my eyes. Then I have to sneeze. Covering my face with both hands, I make a sound, like the short sharp flush of an aeroplane toilet. If my cell mate decides to get shirty I could be done for, I wouldn't be confident of surviving his kind of traditional Chinese face massage.

Right, I'm getting a bit desperate now. Don't like the idea of spending a night in a cell with this drug-crazed criminal. (Although obviously a tiny part of me is still keeping a note of how the anecdote will run.) The chances of it being any kind of set up have all but disappeared. Yes, they've receded well over the bald head of likelihood, and a long way down the hairy back of remote possibility. No, now there's no chance of it being one of Spaz's practical jokes, or Telestar using their links with organised crime to punish me for not signing with them. None at all.

There's that drip again.

Unexploded Munitions

January 2001: Wessex helicopter hovering
above the South Atlantic

The door is wide open and the noise is deafening. The slate grey sea below is ... nasty. For a moment the rugged beauty of the place is upstaged by the niggling fear of sudden death. Instinctively though, I return Simpson's thumbs up. We're going high, really high, for a helicopter. Wish I hadn't agreed to this now, but last night it was difficult to say 'no' to our drunken but enthusiastic hosts who are also trained killers.

They've certainly been showing us around the Falklands. Before, all I knew about this place was the War, penguins and bad weather. And that's all there is, but it takes two days to get here so you can't really go straight home. Besides there's the small matter of several shows to do for the troops.

It's me, Mike Xanadu the impressionist, Tony Tundass as MC, and four dancing girls. Guess which act the seven thousand isolated men like the best? But they can't get their hands on them after the show, so they make do with showing the comedians all their elaborate drinking venues.

Thankfully the gigs have gone okay so far. Previously I'd heard tales of battle-fatigued soldiers rushing the stage, or whole platoons of marines stripping naked immediately before the act comes on, just to psyche them out. But I survive by picking on the officers – at least the squaddies are well behaved when they're present, because as an audience (despite the Geneva Convention) these guys don't take any prisoners. And why should they? They have a real life or death job.

We're in cloud now, which is a little easier to cope with, as at least now you can imagine that you might not be far from the ground. Or in a steamy sauna, or part of an elaborate stage entrance for a Prince concert.

We arrive by Hercules via Brize Norton and Ascension Island. The Falklands are moss green, and from the air remind me of the sort of battle layout a nine-year-old boy might make from papier-mâché and fuzzy felt, for his toy soldiers. Probably won't mention that to the real soldiers though. It's fantastically exciting to be here in a way, but then the facts are that I'm five thousand miles from home surrounded by ocean and men with guns, and all I have to defend myself is some words arranged in a certain order.

A Lieutenant Simpson is our chaperone, a decent Sandhurst sort of chap who says things like 'listen up', 'roger' and 'the show is at twenty-one hundred hours but you might want to check your equipment, and then get some R and R'.

It's as if we're Special Forces come to do a dangerous mission, and in a way, we are. This place is really a very long way away, and it seems preposterous that Britain should lay any sort of claim to it. Probably won't mention that either though, not with all their friends in those cemeteries. Is my country brave, stubborn or just stupid to have all these lives and hardware out here in the middle of the Atlantic?

I don't know whether to feel sorry for the dancing girls or not. They don't do anything more than gyrate to irrelevant pop tracks, and they're very well protected after the shows, but the squaddies all yelp and whistle at them like shepherds with rabies. Are they hapless victims desperate for the money, or just patriotic lasses doing their bit and loving every minute of the attention? Perhaps it's all just gloriously honest.

Being a soldier seems to be a hard but simple existence. The planes, jeeps and huts are all stripped back to their bare essentials, what you see is what you get. No room for enigmatic artists with mood swings here; the army way is one of straightforwardness in every department. March! Fight! Letch! But like reading a book or seeing a film that people have recommended a little too much, I'm finding it difficult to make conversation with the dancers.

What if the engine cuts out? Helicopters don't have spares do they? One of the dancing girls is distressed. Can't hear her over the noise. All four squaddies race across to offer a shoulder to cry on. Oh good I don't feel so bad now. But if I start to blub they might not be so sympathetic.

Oh yes, Tundass has a serviceable act now. All clichés and well worn ideas but he knows how to press the right buttons. His skin was always thick enough to keep going. He loves the drinking here too. He and Xanadu have been out all three nights so far, but I've had to surrender halfway through each campaign and go back to my bunk. (Which is literally a bunk, but thankfully, no one's in the top one.)

Xanadu's impressions are going down very well. Even before he gets to the joke, there's a round of applause as they simply recognise the voice. Straight stand-ups like myself are jealous of this alchemy. It's like an ordinary bloke producing the keys of a Porsche halfway through a disco – it unbalances the playing field a little. But impersonations are magical, even if they do tend to hang on the repeated premise of celebrities and their catch-phrases in unfamiliar situations. Even off stage Xanadu just can't stop. If we're in a jeep he has to be Jeremy Clarkson, if we see a beach it's Churchill. The best response he gets in the show is when he does the other officers – and he only met them a few days ago.

The officers' mess has pictures of famous battles on the wall. Goose Green, D-Day, Waterloo. It all reminds me of the photos of past successes on the walls at Rushwood Studios.

If I die when this helicopter crashes perhaps they'll build a memorial – a stone column on top of a windy tor, and on it a brass plate 'Jerome Stevens – he always went down well'.

Yesterday they took us on a boat trip. About half a mile out in the wind and the rain, we stopped. Then a corporal pulls out a grenade shaped object, which turns out to be a GRENADE!

'Take cover' calls Simpson as if he were a guard on a train shouting 'Mind the doors'. Over the side it goes and sure enough a few seconds later there's a huge 'bang'. Tony cheers belatedly as we're covered with spray. There's definitely something wrong with him – I'm just glad to be in one piece. No need to do that again eh lads? But then the boat heads off towards the middle of the explosion.

'Flipping Nora' says Tony as if we're in a war film with John Mills and we've just sunk a U-boat. But instead of Germans, it turns out we've killed hundreds of fish, which are now all slowly rising to the surface, and a nameless corporal is already scooping them into a plastic crate at the back of the boat. Only now I feign some sort of glee, but it's more relief that we've still got all our limbs.

Back at the jetty, as they're unloading and having a cigarette someone notices a few pilot whales that have beached a couple of hundred yards away. There's an icy wind but I have to go and have a look – how often do you get a chance like this? The others don't bother.

Back home this story would finish every news bulletin and the RSPCA would be putting in overtime. Here it means nothing. The whales are further away than they look. Six giant black truncheons, mini nuclear submarines laid out on the sand. As I approach there's a hissing sound, one of them is still alive, I wasn't expecting that. What do you do, what do you say? It's all too much and I jog back to the others, but now I can't seem to find them.

Did I take a wrong turn? Where've they gone? Not the best place to get lost, out here in the wind and the rain. All my survival training has been carried out in warm rooms with drinks and meal vouchers thrown in. Perhaps I could do an 'after dinner' for a colony of seals – I can already hear them clapping their flippers together and honking for more. No, this is serious now, the light is fading, I don't fancy a freezing night stumbling over minefields and unburied Argentinean dead.

'HOO HAA!' suddenly shouts a voice from behind a rock, and Xanadu emerges 'Tony put me up to it' he continues, as Al Pacino. Then the rest of the camouflaged party appear round the side of another huge rock. Tundass is wild eyed and animated, 'We got you Stevens, we got you!' The soldiers laugh a little sheepishly, and then pull out more cigarettes.

Of course, Membury Services all those years ago, I drove off and left him, Tundass was unlikely to forget. Well at least they didn't desert me here, this isn't quite the same as just somewhere near Swindon. (Later I find out that, actually, Tundass was quite keen to leave me there.)

The whole trip has had a surreal quality and I've felt guilty for forgetting about Suzy for a while, and I suppose that's why those whales were too much. Last night I got chatting to a Scottish Sergeant whose wife, it turned out, had died of cancer. He was glad to talk about it and he kept on empathising, 'Och it's a fuckin' evil disease' again and again.

At one point there were tears in his eyes. Not the conversation I was expecting in this place, and not the sort of thing you mention in the morning either.

This is definitely another experience rather than fun. But there are worse places I could be. Oh yes, Lt Simpson has already asked if I'd be interested in going to Iraq or Afghanistan.

If I survive this I'm probably going to be completely deaf.

We're supposed to go home tomorrow – the end of another trip. After four shows and three nights of drinking our motley company have formed a bond. Indeed Xanadu keeps informing me in his best Leslie Phillips 'ding dong' tones that he has made more than a connection with one of the dancers.

But we've all literally faced an army together and I don't think we've had any casualties. Difficult to explain to anyone else, the jokes are almost irrelevant. You had to be there. A successful mission all round and next week will feel flat by comparison.

But flat is good when you're ten thousand feet up. We've been hovering for a while, the pilot stabilising the chopper each time it takes a sudden cuff from the wind. Now Simpson is shouting at me. He's motioning that we should take off our safety belts!

'WHY THE HELL WOULD I DO THAT?'

He must be joking, or are we in trouble? Am I the only one without a parachute? But he's smiling and everyone else has taken off theirs. Tundass is the first, now he's coming over to help me. Alright, alright. Gingerly I undo my belt.

Simpson shouts something to the pilot. Then, horrifyingly, the engine stops. We're all going to die, the helicopter's dropping. Slowly at first, then much quicker. We're in freefall. There's a terrible eerie whistling sound. We're definitely all going to die. God help me. Hang on . . . the others are smiling, and floating. My feet are off the ground! We're all weightless! Floating in space! I can't quite bring myself to smile though. Please turn the engine back on. But I'm still flying. Tundass is laughing like a moron.

At last the engine chugs into life with a roar. And we come down to the helicopter floor with a bump. Now I can smile. We're still alive. I wish they'd told me they were going to do that.

Keep Clear

September 2001: Running through Hyde Park

The air is damp and freezing black, with a hint of burnt leaves. Normally I wouldn't cut through Hyde Park at night, partly because I don't want to get mugged, but mainly because it's not really a short cut between anywhere. Raising my hands above my head I run down the path.

I'm alive.

'I'm aaaliiive!' I shout as I run, just in case there's any doubt.

It's a big charity dinner for children dying of AIDS, and I'm happy to do it, but the fact that three days ago two passenger jets flew in to the side of the World Trade Centre in New York isn't exactly going to lighten the mood. So, just to recap I mustn't mention children, death, hospitals, aeroplanes, America, hijacks, the Middle East or any other disaster that occurs between now and then. Excellent.

The crowd is well turned out and probably feel they've done their bit by just being here. It's all bow ties and designer dresses. Unable to bear sitting through the meal I pace up and down in the corridor outside. There I meet Zafira again, who's roped me into it. She's wearing a deep pink satin dress which rolls back her 50 odd years. She kisses me on both cheeks and then wipes some lipstick off my face with the corner of a hanky like a Mum. It's a strangely intimate moment.

'Thanks so much for doing this Jerome, it means so much to me with Sebastian and everything.'

I nod understandingly, but I've no idea who she's talking about.

'We need to laugh in these dark days' she says.

Wow, now I'm really in the mood.

Back in the ballroom everything's a bit muted. The events of September the 11th have shocked everyone. Eventually the toastmaster calls the whispering tables to order and suggests a two-minute silence. 'After all there's an unoccupied table here sponsored by United Airlines.' There's an audible gasp but it turns out they're not dead, just didn't fancy flying at the moment.

There are some sniffles during the silence. Thank goodness I don't have to follow that, there's someone else on first. But he turns out to be the father of a seven-year-old haemophiliac who's just died of AIDS. Brilliant, just really . . . brilliant. He speaks eloquently for 10 minutes on the nature of grief. Hooray. Now there's not a dry eye in the house. (Is this a set up?) A tiny part of me admires his bravery, but by far the largest part of me is thinking 'SHUT UP YOU BURK, I'M ON NEXT!'

Oh, and it turns out that Sebastian is a son that Zafira lost to AIDS two years ago. Of course he is.

Please Mr Toastmaster do a bit in between – a song, a trick, a racist mother in-law joke, anything. Can this get any worse? Oh great now he's mentioned the Trade Centre again, that'll cheer them up. You may as well introduce me by saying 'Speaking of heinous acts . . .' but it's much straighter than that.

'My Lords, Ladies and Gentlemen . . . Jerome Stevens!'

Dead man walking!

Standing now in the middle of the park. The earth is soft, the fog is thick and summer is almost unimaginable.

The doctors have officially given up on Suzy. She can eat what she wants now, and do whatever she can. They say we can only make her comfortable. But how comfortable can you be on death row? Was all that nasty chemo worth it? Well, it could have been. But it wasn't.

Nothing for two minutes. I keep grinning, struggling to keep my timing in the absence of any laughter. Come on! If Suzy can get through chemo then I can get through this. Eventually there are a few titters. It's rolling now and I even survive mentioning aeroplane food. Come on, follow me! But even when I think I have them, they're very fragile, falling silent at any hint of a pause. Just keep on hammering them. After a very long 15 minutes I'm almost getting normal reactions. It's like smacking the end of a glass ketchup bottle again and again, until at last it splurges onto the plate.

That's what the colour of Zafira's dress reminded me of. A pink felt pen I used to own. Suzy and I both got a bumper pack each, from some relative. Suzy used hers to win second prize in a Post Office competition, but I took mine to pieces, tried to make some pan pipes, then got sent to bed early.

Standing in a park in the middle of London the nearest lights are further away than you might think. There's an occasional car horn. My only motivation to move is a creeping chill. I despair for Suzy. It's just not fair that's all. The whole thing is crooked and unjust.

About to wind up now, I can see the finish line. Just then a baby cries. A baby!? But ... this is bad. Wylie Coyote has just climbed back up a cliff-face only to find the whole thing about to crumble and crash into the valley below.

You see I've had run-ins with the under fives before, at festivals and the odd lunch time cabaret. It's a no-win situation. You can't exactly engage them in conversation, or even tell them to be quiet. Everyone takes the side of the infant. Deep breath.

'Ah, it's a baby!' I say.

The proud father stands up and rocks her a little.

'What's the name?'

'Maisy.'

'And how old is Maisy?'

'Seven and a half months.'

Now I'm going to gamble everything.

'And . . . you thought she'd enjoy this evening did you . . . ?'

It's a risk, but suddenly there's a huge laugh. It seems that, just as I'd hoped, Maisy's squawks have annoyed others as well. Yes, I've tapped into a great big artesian well of tension! Maisy squeals again and her father takes her out. Plain sailing now. Time to get off.

A couple of minutes then 'That's all from me, thank you, goodnight!' Genuine applause. Got there in the end, but I don't want to hang around, I have to go and run in the frost.

Just then my phone rings. It's Zafira. Apparently I'm 'marvellous'. She says she thought they might be a tricky crowd. (Although when I arrived she said they'd be a 'lovely crowd'. Nervous promoters often pull that one.)

And do I want to come back to hers for fondue and schnapps? It's not just the way Zafira looks that is seductive; it's her whole way of doing things. That time I went to her place before; she drove us there in an old Volvo (chic and charismatic) but the number plate was 'L-O-O . . .' something. Now, on her car that seemed charming, even stylish. But if it had belonged to Tundass, for instance, the whole thing would have seemed more like a mobile toilet. It's like jokes, I suppose – there's often a thin line between a good and bad one, it's more to do with the way in which it's done, the spirit of the person behind it.

Anyway, I decline. Tonight's a night for going home, locking the door and checking the children are all still breathing.

Prison ⦀⦀⦀ ⦀⦀⦀ ⦀⦀⦀

They say parenthood is a rollercoaster, but let's hope that at the end, they don't present us with a photo of the moment we were the most terrified, like they do at a theme park. Stepping out of the bath onto something soft and warm, or on being handed a megaphone by the police to talk your son into letting the hostages go from the staff room.

But I like being a Dad, I've even got a 'Dad costume', a shabby cardigan with elbow patches to dig children in the ribs with, to cajole them into eating vegetables or to help them get my crazy jokes. It goes with my paint splattered T-shirts and trainers from the eighties. Sometimes I put them all on, and go out on my sensible bike with its straight handlebars and box tied on the back to carry tools and shopping in. This is exercise and leisure time; released from bringing home the bacon.

'What's for lunch?' I shout as I bash open the gate with my front wheel.

'Did you get the bacon?' Marita replies, and then I turn round in one, and head off back towards the shops. I knew I'd forgotten something.

Later I shuffle round the house tutting at the television, and refusing to help with homework, mainly because I know that if I do I'll be horribly out of my depth. Sometimes I even watch my wife doing odd jobs about the house. At last, when they're all in bed, I lock up and then go and squeeze the last bit out of the oldest toothpaste.

It's not easy – of course it isn't. Don't tell them, but they each have the power to destroy you. To take a knife and plunge it into your heart and then jump up and down on your slumped body, and that's to say nothing of the emotional hurt they can cause.

Yes, sometimes it's all horribly out of control. Like when we visited that stately home and sheltered from the rain in the butterfly house, and the boys just ran around trying to stamp them all to death.

You might be able to cope with one child, but when there are many it's like native American tribes to be subdued in the New World – just when you think you've reached a treaty with one, the other will creep up behind and try to burn down the fort you've been holding.

But sometimes, though, I can't help feeling I've sold my kids short: that many of the presents I've bought them are the type that will be broken by Boxing Day; that I've always been too keen to please and too afraid to give them things that are practical, things that might be considered dull. Not enough holidays in chilly England building rafts on islands, and far far too much television. (Once when Stan was two he woke up in the night and shouted 'car insurance'!)

Perhaps my choice of career hasn't made it so easy for them to see past the shallowness of celebrity-culture. But those shiny lights, they suck you in. Once doing an after-dinner slot at a science fiction convention I met the guest of honour, an ageing actress who had been in two episodes of the original series of *Star Trek*. She gently took my hand and introduced herself 'Jennifer Lansdowne – Princess of Triskellon'. Part of me was staggered that a grown woman could evidently make a whole career out of only a fortnight's work, but another part of me was thinking – oh yeah, I remember that episode! As I say, it sucks you in.

What if I really don't make it out of this cell? I should compose a letter. My idea-pad is still in my pocket, and I have a pen from the hotel. There's no guarantee of them ever getting this but . . . after a few minutes I have edited my thoughts.

Dear children,

Since the moment each of you was born I have been proud to be your Dad. I hope that one day you too will be proud of me, even though I spent a lot of time in pubs and probably died in prison.

Perhaps this needs explaining. As you know my job was to make people laugh. Sometimes this was fun; sometimes it was a bit dangerous. But looking back, I think I made one main mistake, and that was trying a bit too hard to become rich and famous. Obviously this didn't really work. But I know now, that I was already rich, and famous with the only audience that really mattered. You lot. You never failed to shout 'rubbish' when I was rubbish and often we laughed together like friends. You also need to know that I laughed at your jokes too, and even stole your material a few times.

Sure I would like to have been able to buy us all more treats and made you more proud of me, but just maybe then we wouldn't have known why we all loved each other so much.

Boys, never ever give up! Listen to your Mum – well more than I did. Marita, sorry about all this . . .

The pen's stopped working now, and tears are streaming down my face.

Beware

August 2002: Walking to the plane
at Edinburgh Airport

I've just been up in Edinburgh for a few days to have a look around. I don't have to do the Fringe anymore. Sure I picked up a gig or two but I'm glad to be going back home. Besides I've just seen the best show ever.

All around are frontless shops full of magazines, sunglasses and continental adaptors. From time to time there are loud but woolly announcements by a woman who sounds as if she's locked in a cupboard with a microphone and a glockenspiel.

An attic room at five past midnight: for the next three and a half weeks this pokey little space at the top of an obscure Edinburgh college will be described as a 'venue' in the Fringe programme. Now it's jammed with 43 chairs, that all seem to need fixing. It's the sort of room that in term time is probably used to store chairs that need fixing.

With three minutes to go, there are only five punters here. Every time there's a noise we all look round towards the door, yearning for people to join us and dilute our vulnerability.

It's the first night of the Festival and Spaz and I are here to see a preview of Tony Tundass' show (because he begged us). He's learnt how to survive on the club circuit all right, but this year he's seeking critical acclaim and has bought a ticket for the great Scottish lottery.

At the end of our row there's a middle-aged woman with a walking stick. She's wearing a sensible navy jumper and I expect she owns a Labrador. Three rows behind is a Japanese looking man who's clearly in the wrong place. In the front row is Tristan Watson from *The Times* – the reason why Tundass was so desperate to fill the place up.

Perhaps I should buy a book to read on the plane. Or write one. *Seven Easy Steps to Being a Millionaire*. Step one: undercut the competition, write *Six Easy Steps to Being a Millionaire*. Where do all those quotes on the back come from? 'Magnificent', 'A masterpiece', 'The must read book of the year'. Never 'Pretty cover, but a bit long' or 'Once I put it down I couldn't pick it up'. But thinking about it, they're just like quotes on posters at the Fringe. Quotes that adorn the walls, like texts in a church, to help you believe the impossible.

Spaz is drunk and talking too loudly over the pre-show music. I wish we hadn't come now. Too late: the lights are dimming: here we go. The 'Rocky' music – from the film: not a good start. Bit of a cliché. Tundass comes on in a large brown homemade costume.

'Good evening everyone, I'm Rocky!'

We are all silent.

'Oh . . . he's a rock!' says Spaz out loud. Then he and I guffaw at the hopelessness of the opening.

Tundass is encouraged though. 'Anyway I've just been playing Scissor Paper Stone, but people seem to be able to guess what I'm going to be . . .'

He waits for a laugh that doesn't come.

'A rock!' Spaz says matter of fact. There are a few chuckles.

'That's right, a rock.'

Is there some twist to this? Apparently not.

There's a longer pause. Tony has frozen. Tristan Watson begins to write.

Spaz shakes his head and whispers 'An hour of this!' then he buries his head in his hands.

I look up at the ceiling. It's not far away.

You don't stand much of a chance in Edinburgh these days if you don't have your own PR person. Only the very big boys make money up here. Last year friends with successful shows ran up debts of up to £15,000. I've got too much to lose – my reputation, my money, my summer. These days it just seems like a great big scam.

Sideways I catch a glimpse of the woman leaning forward on her stick with the pained expression of a doctor examining a nasty rash. Behind her the Japanese tourist is grinning without understanding.

By now Tundass has shed his costume and is on to the differences between cats and dogs. Then he continues, 'You know what it's like when your Mum won't give you the keys to the garden shed?'

'What?!' splurts Spaz.

This is supposed to be observational material but he's managed to observe something that possibly no one else has ever experienced in their lives.

Watson is wobbling his leg in boredom. Slowly our forced snorts and chuckles tire, and now under Tony's voice I can actually hear the scratching of the pen that's writing his obituary.

'Flight 94' has an ominous ring to it. As in 'what happened to Flight 94?' Fast forward to anxious relatives waiting in Edinburgh. All the other flights have 'landed' or 'baggage in hall' next to their name. A member of staff whispers 'lost radar contact over Manchester'. A man in a kilt breaks down.

Eventually I slyly angle my watch to catch a glimpse of the time with a minimum of movement. Ten minutes to go.

Just then Tundass stops and sighs. Did he notice me looking at my watch?

'What are you writing?' he snaps at Watson.

Surely he recognises him. Maybe not.

'A review for the *The Times*' Watson replies.

Tony's eyebrows rise in exaggerated dismay, like Tower Bridge before a boat goes through.

'Bugger, you hate me don't you?'

Watson keeps writing.

Tundass begins to undo his trousers. 'What's he doing?' I mutter.

Spaz looks bemused. Watson hasn't noticed yet. The woman begins to laugh disconcertingly.

Tony's down to his boxers but there's something else attached to his torso.

'A suicide belt!' laughs Spaz.

And so it is. Complete with candles instead of dynamite. That's quite a funny idea. I hope they're candles.

Watson looks up. It's the first genuine laugh of the night, from the rest of us. The critic smiles ruefully.

'I don't care now!' says Tundass. 'We can all go together. How many stars will that get? Eh? How many stars will you give me in your review if I blow us all up? What if I blow *you* up?'

He's milking this a bit now.

'EH!' Tundass shouts this right into Watson's face. He seems determined to commit suicide one way or the other.

'Easy Tony' says Spaz ironically.

'And you two can shut the fuck up as well!'

'Calm down' says Spaz. 'Listen, I used to be a hostage negotiator. Well, I phoned them up and they said they didn't have any vacancies, but I kept them talking . . . and they gave me a job!'

Spaz gets the biggest laugh of the night. This isn't difficult, but it's a little bit unforgivable. But we're all a bit tense and it's Spaz, so he gets away with it.

Tundass is still glaring at Watson who in turn tries to stare him out.

'Can we have a show please' says the woman with an Edinburgh lilt.

'SHUT UP. DO YOU WANT ME TO PULL THIS?'

Tony is holding a black cord.

'This is ridiculous' says the woman. And she heaves herself up on her stick.

'I'm warning you' says Tony. In a more measured tone.

Watson spins round, he looks nervous. The woman sits down. This is really unexpectedly heavy. What's he going to do? Kill us all in a glorious blaze of publicity that will overshadow the festival for years to come. Probably not. But he's always been a bit unstable. There's definitely a small chance.

'What are you going to do Tony?' I say as calmly as possible.

He just shakes his head and says nothing. Maybe he's cracking up.

Another few seconds pass. We can hear the noise of the bars and the traffic outside, and then the distant laughter of the venue below. They're having a *good* time.

Things take longer now. 9/11 has affected everything.

Put all your metal things in a tray. They should cover them with a tea towel and you should only get back the ones you can remember.

Everyone knows where they were when it happened. Except me, I was delirious with flu.

Apparently that same night Spaz tried something on stage about playing giant Jenga in New York. He had to run from the building he says. But I'm not sure I believe him so much these days. Fact and fantasy are beginning to blur.

'Right. That's enough' says the woman. 'This is appalling! I'm off.'

She gets up.

'DON'T GO!' screams Tony. Then it all happens very quickly.

There's a bang. At first I think she has fallen over some chairs, but she doesn't get up. Then I turn round and Tony is holding a gun.

'You've killed her!' shouts Watson. 'You've *killed* her!'

Tundass just stares at the floor.

'Please let me go!' he pleads with Tundass.

'What, so you can write a bad review?'

'I won't write a bad review. I won't write any review. I swear it.'

'You'll tell the police?'

'No I won't.'

'Of course you will. You're a liar. Aren't you? Say you're a liar. Say you are a liar!

'I'm a liar. Listen, I have a baby. Please let me go.'

'Clap me.'

'. . . what?'

None of us can quite believe this is happening. We'd better not take any chances though. All those years of derision built up. He's always been mad.

'Clap me!' he says again, this time with a smile.

I don't notice at first, but then the woman in the jumper gets up off the floor and joins Tony on stage. They both take a bow. Spaz roars with laughter. We've been had. When we realise we start clapping.

'You Bastard!' shouts Spaz, then claps with his hands above his head.

Duty Free. Which reminds you of all the people you have a duty to buy a present for. Perfumes they won't wear, liqueurs they won't drink and Toblerones they won't be able to eat without hurting their mouths.

The crew is all in orange. At the desk a human satsuma picks up the tannoy. It's hard to ignore everyone's desperation to get on board. A bit like the Fringe.

'Would you like a newspaper?'

'No thanks I have a book to write. *The Bluffer's Guide to Parachuting.*'

'38F, halfway along on the left.'

38F the cursed seat. That familiar thin metallic smell, like someone doing the ironing. Dirt will soon be collecting in the corners of our nostrils – tiny pyramids of gravel, that we'll have to find a way to secretly excavate.

A window seat. From the outside we must look like we're trapped in a row of washing machines at the launderette.

Stumpy little trucks buzz about the tarmac. A lorry with a flight of stairs on the back, leading nowhere. That's my career, that is. Perhaps, I feel more like that burnt out plane over there, at the edge of the runway – the one they say they use for fire practice.

Watson slumps in his chair. We applaud long and loud. Tundass smiles and shouts 'Louder', milking it now in a slightly undignified way. But it's his finest moment, even if we're all equally impressed and relieved. When the noise dies down we gather round the stage.

'This is Muriel. We were at drama school together' explains Tony.

'Lovely to meet you' she says with an actressy voice. She's younger than I thought.

Just then the Japanese tourist breaks into the circle and gives Tundass a card. 'Mike Zatopek, Walt Disney Corporation. Just loved the show.'

Spaz and I laugh again. It's what Tony deserves tonight. Meanwhile Tristan Watson has gathered his things and scuttled out of the room, out of the venue and, if he's got any sense, out of the city. Within a few hours the story will be round every bar in town.

Stop!

The N7 hoovers through West London sucking up the capital's human bits and pieces after a night of partying. The laughter is loud amongst the groups of friends, and some teenage girls have started singing Robbie Williams' 'Angels'.

'She offers me protection, a lot of love and affection.'

A few others are asleep, and one or two are obviously on their way home after a night shift, tolerating the rest. The driver, too, looks beleaguered and makes quick time between the stops on the empty roads. Now the girls are in full swing, singing 'I'm loving angels instead!'

Upstairs at the front, I'm feeling indignantly self-righteous. Tonight I did another benefit. After the event I'm usually glad to have helped, but at the time these shows can often be a lot more trouble than the ones you get paid for. Despite meticulous planning and making sure the acts all turn up unnecessarily early, there may be an awkward atmosphere. Alternatively they can be really fun. I remember Spaz coming on for the second half of something for a terminal disease and announcing 'Good news everyone, we've cured it – you can all go home'.

Besides who wouldn't like to be able to give to charity and then be quite literally applauded for it?

However this one's for the Jevons Cancer Trust and I didn't want to turn it down. It's in a big West End theatre too. A muggy Victorian labyrinth of pokey rooms and concrete stairs all coated with the sweet smell of dust. On the other side of the curtain, it opens out into a huge black void, the slope of the stage sucking you towards the orchestra pit. But when this place is full, and on your side, 15 minutes of material can last for 20. Thousands of tiny pale orbs focused in your direction, and when the laughs come, they roll and roll. And they did.

But as I chat to Arnie Zoot in the Green Room about a new gig in Prague, there's a flurry of activity amongst the organisers who are all wearing red T-shirts.

'We've got a special surprise guest' one of them beams.

At the time I affect disinterest but the next thing I know, I'm standing at the back of the stalls waiting to see who it is.

'Ladies and Gentlemen' booms the off stage microphone. 'Mickey Spinola!'

My stomach turns, and the hair stands up on the back of my neck. There's a huge cheer – after all he's 'off the telly'. The first couple of lines I don't recognise. The third is a new twist on an old pub gag about a blind man and the wrong guide dog. Then, clear as a bell, there's one of Danny Bullen's jokes. Nothing added, nothing taken away (and Danny hasn't got many to spare!). It's like watching a DVD you're not sure is pirated, then all of a sudden the silhouette of someone carrying popcorn walks across the screen. Now I'm walking towards the stage. Oh and there's a line of mine! Two of mine! In the same order as I use them. Right down at the front now.

'Why don't you use your own gags?' I hear myself shouting.

There's a gap. He's thrown for a second.

'Where did you come from . . . ?' he stumbles '. . . I don't interrupt you when you're at work and say . . .'

'. . . Do you want fries with that' I butt in, completing the well worn put down. The audience laughs.

'Yeah . . .' Spinola carries on, 'I mean what do you use for contraception . . .'

'. . . My personality!?' I say pre-empting his insult, and getting the laugh again.

Now there is desperation in his eyes and sweat is breaking out on his forehead. He won't have any original ideas for dealing with hecklers, but he has one last go.

'Isn't it a shame . . .'

'. . . When cousins marry!' I shout.

The audience thinks I'm a stooge and that we're some sort of double act. Spinola's eyes are darting about now, like ball bearings in an aerosol can. Now I'm walking up the steps at the side of the stage.

'Give me the microphone and no one will get hurt' I say.

'S-s-security!' he shouts.

'Your Mum's in the Stalls!' I reply.

Huge laugh. Then he drops the mic. and runs. The audience cheer and applaud. A long loud applause, some of them even get to their feet.

Then a male voice begins to sing over the top of the clapping. A loud eerie descant, which gets louder and louder. Opening my eyes, I'm still in prison and Bruce Leak is singing to himself.

Prison ⊞⊞ ⊞⊞ ⊞⊞ I

B ruce is clearly at home here. Well, more than I am. You wouldn't catch me singing. Our eyes meet, but he carries on crooning in Cantonese. I'm tempted to try and join in but I don't want him to think I'm making fun of him. He must be still drunk. Eventually he finishes. I applaud as sincerely as possible. He just stares back. Now, I clear my throat and launch out.

'Once I was afraid, I was petrified, kept thinking I could never live without you by my side, but I spent so many nights wondering how you did me wrong that I grew strong, learnt how to get along.'

'Sa ya back! . . .' Bruce joins in. Thrown for a second, I carry on.

'. . . From outer space! La la la la la la la la.'

It's a mess but we're both still singing.

I've no idea what the next bit is, but I try and keep the tune up and get to the chorus.

'la la la . . . I've got all my life to live, I've got all my love to give and I WILL SURVIVE!'

'Aw Wi Suvi!' shouts Bruce and then we both shout it again together. A hint of a smile crosses his face. I wonder where he learnt that. Some Karaoke bar before he got sacked for drinking the bar stocks? Mustn't lose this momentum. I know . . .

'I should be so lucky! Lucky lucky! Lucky!'

'Dancing Queen, only 17, da de da . . .'

No, something he might know. Everybody was Kung Fu Fighting? Maybe not.'

I'm running out of confidence and he's beginning to look at me as if this impromptu sing-along is some sort of psychological torture. Back to awkward silence.

A couple of minutes' later he's asleep again. Did that just happen?

No Stopping
At Any Time

December 2002: Going nowhere at all

D arkness falls upon the room. The audience utter their first collective noise – an 'oooh' of anticipation. The music starts, the disco lights spin round, and now there are cheers and screams. Four comics stand unmoved at the back of the room. The MC is desperately trying to work up some adrenaline by throwing a few shadow punches before he has to go on stage. 'Good luck everybody' he mouths and then he's off parading through the crowd.

This is the 13th night of 21 Christmas shows in Nottingham. Let's get this over with. Christmas crowds are the worst.

Before the MC speaks, someone shouts something. One group at the back laughs.

'What was that?'

No one will repeat it. This is a bad start. Not being given a chance to deal with that has lost him some authority. Tonight they're all wearing hats, and have been drinking since lunchtime. The boss has paid for this so they've invested nothing personally and most seem reluctant to venture far from the free bar. We need to fix bayonets and get ready for hand-to-hand combat. Divide and conquer. Lob, smash: lob, smash: lob, smash.

Relax everyone: he's found an American. Crowd and performer unite in the triumph of discovering a scapegoat.

It's difficult not to despise a crowd like this – if they talk during the show, try and draw attention to themselves, or laugh at swearwords just because they're swearwords. Each party will also contain two or three who wish they weren't there at all. Wives, boyfriends, colleagues, each hoping that they can stay for just the minimum amount of time necessary. Me too.

The MC stands in front of the herd of seated wildebeests. He tries to strike a deal – you be nice to us we'll make you laugh. He neglects to mention that we'll be assuming that they'll all be able to follow basic logic. But then what would be the point? Besides, like so many other shows advertised as a comedy night, to the management at least, this evening is more about selling beer.

As I mount the stage the MC shakes my hand and gives me a knowing look as he passes on the poisoned baton. We're off.

On waking this morning I held the moment, deliberately not reminding myself of where I was, trying to work out what I felt about the day ahead. Nothing. For a second, the half-forgotten smell of a holiday cottage. No, this is many years later. A damp hotel in a damp place, the rain driving sideways at a window 14 floors up.

I also have the beginnings of a sore throat, the only consolation of which is that with an American accent I can now sound like the bloke who does the 'coming soon' ads at the cinema. You know, the one who speaks in a continual belch. Perhaps with this in mind, at around midday I make my way to the Multiplex at the edge of town. Just like yesterday and the day before.

Someone walks across my line of vision with a jug of beer.

BOO! I shout into the mic. She spills some. Cheers and applause. Is this what my job has come to? Shouting at girls to make them drop things?

I haven't written anything new for ages. Yes, thinking about it, I did pretty much the same set last December. There's a creeping staleness in my act, like a rock-hard Christmas cake that gets brought out year after year. Enthusiasm for the job is directly related to having new material, which in turn is related to freshness of performance. But writing new stuff these days is like winkling coins out of a piggy bank through the slot in the top. And I have this niggling fear that I should really smash the whole thing up and start over again.

A group at the back are talking. I try to eyeball them. But if I dare to let them in, my planned words might all unravel.

Before spending a few days away, you imagine you'll fill your time with useful tasks and hours of inspired writing. But as soon you arrive, any zap of creativity seems earthed by the spongy hotel carpet. Besides, Nottingham doesn't exactly meet you halfway. It has a one-way system and a shopping centre just like everywhere else.

My best stab at local material is 'I met Robin Hood yesterday. He was taking from the rich and giving to the poor. Okay, he said *Big Issue!*'.

It works but it's nothing I'm proud of.

The 2.10 showing of *Insomnia* starring Al Pacino and Robin Williams. Let's hope I don't fall asleep. Entering the auditorium carrying a Coke, it's suddenly dark between trailers, and I stumble down a step, reeling sideways into a hidden row of seats, which catch me full in the groin. Thrown to the floor, as the breath is knocked out of me, just like in a cartoon, I writhe uncontrollably on the ground for a second or two and then struggle to my knees to save face, spilling my drink down my arm. But there's no need to try, the dim light from the next trailer reveals an entirely empty auditorium. Slowly I slump back to the floor, resting my head on the tacky carpet.

The adverts crackle on, and now the sound of classical music is all around in stereo. Then the rasp of the real 'coming soon' man: 'Coming soon . . . a row of seats you weren't expecting . . .'

Then in the gap before the next ad, I can hear the faint rumblings of the film in the screen next door. A car chase and some gunshots, or is it just the distant sound of Nottingham?

On arrival in the stuffy venue this evening I feel like I'm coming down with flu. But I'm on first, so at least I'll get it over with. But I'll also be first to draw the hecklers.

Clever stuff is going for nothing, but making fun of individuals is going well of course. Let's churn out our nastiest greatest hits for 15 minutes and not a second longer. At least no one will remember this.

Now I can't help drifting up above myself, looking down and wondering how hard I would have to kick the head of the man in the front row – who is talking – before it would come off completely. Need a holiday.

Racing through my stuff, leaving no gaps. But now a woman is shouting. I ignore her – she looks like trouble – until just before then end.

'Okay, what's your name and what do you?'

'I'm Edith and I organised this whole party.'

The crowd groan. Many of them seem all too familiar with Edith, from work presumably.

'Well you didn't organise it very well . . .' I retort. '. . . there are a couple of empty chairs over there.'

Edith's mouth drops open, she takes a deep breath, then lets out a howl and collapses sobbing onto the ashtrays and remains of party poppers on the table, her yellow paper hat bobbing up and down in time to the sobs. No one is sober enough even to pretend to comfort her, a few laugh and one bald man even raises his glass. There's nothing else to say, I've done my time and besides I've nearly lost my voice.

'Well all that remains for me to do is wish you all a very happy Christmas' I rasp with pointless irony.

The rest of the show passes in a similar vein. There's nothing creative about what we do tonight, we just get through it.

It would be dangerous to give up doing live work – you lose sharpness and it becomes too easy to kid yourself about what you're writing. But I'm not sure there's an escape route anymore.

Last night, after the show, while bored and burning up, I watched one of those 'Top One Hundred Greatest . . .' programmes. This one was about sitcoms. While obviously being an excuse to show lots of old clips, it got me thinking that the actual top seven or eight were more likely in some TV exec's waste paper bin.

In showbiz, stand-up is invariably seen as a stepping-stone to what you really want to do. What does that make us – those who are still at it all these years later? The in-betweens – students always on a gap year, manual workers who started on the shop floor . . . and stayed there. I've hit the wall. So many nights, so many names, so many faces.

The show's over and the acts stand around the bar absent-mindedly watching the disco. I can't dance anymore, the tooth fairy's older cousin who steals hair and enthusiasm has had my dancing shoes long ago. Tonight the audience seems to be full mostly of people like Edith, all thinking that if we were any good we would be famous by now. Maybe they're right.

'Apparently Spaz has got a series off Channel 4' says the newish comic who's name I can't remember.

'Really!?' I spin round. Why didn't he tell me I wonder? Well he's like that – lives in his own world.

'That's great,' I say. 'He deserves it'.

And he does, good for him. There are two types who go on to greater things, the absurdly lucky and the totally deserving. No one will quibble with Spaz's big break. We toast his good health.

Now there's a middle-aged man hanging about at the end of the bar. Oh oh, I spy another 'What should I do with some scripts

I've written' conversation coming towards me. Not tonight please. Tonight I'd just say 'Cut out the middle man, put them all in the bin'. Must scurry to the loo.

Swaying, I stand in the cubicle steadying myself on a cistern. The air-vent in the window is clogged with grey dust, and it looks how I feel. The floor is far wetter than it should be.

Washing my hands a pale-faced youth with a gold chain nudges me.

'You did alright didn't you!?'

'Thanks.'

'Do you do this full time?'

Sometimes I have a gently rising sense of panic that I might not make it out of burning wrecks like tonight. That this might be as far as I get in my career – that I'm never going to play badminton for England.

'You were the best, mate, no seriously!'

'Thanks.'

Why do they always have to put us in an order?

'We liked the routine about going to Amsterdam best.'

'That wasn't me, that was Andy Smike!'

'No it was you . . . wasn't it?'

'No.'

'Do you know Mickey Spinola?'

It's the last straw and I just walk away.

On my way out I stop between the door to the Gents, and the fire door to the outside corridor – a tiny four by six feet hinterland. I need to get away from that bloke, but I also can't face being on display at the disco either. Trapped between the loo and a hard place. (This was the last time I was in a cell.) 'Sorry Marita, sorry kids, Mum and Dad, sorry Suzy – I was hoping for better than this.'

It's the extremes that are shattering. Acclaim, loneliness: acclaim, loneliness. Like rock that's gradually worn down by the heat of the day and then the chill of the night, except for us it's the other way round. It's another one of those back to the wall moments.

Don't fancy the walk back in the rain to the hotel – slaloming past fights, dropped kebabs and splashes of vomit. Huh, it's all good Baccalaurean fun I suppose. Not that anyone here would understand what that means. You know, Bacchus the Greek god of wine, or is it to do with French exams? – maybe I don't know either. Could always watch telly again back at the hotel – no I'll only see someone I know.

Must phone Ralph, I haven't seen him for ages.

When eventually I return to the edge of the disco there's a wild atmosphere in the room. There could be a fight. Not long after that the bar stops serving alcohol early. That's how bad it is.

Ahead Only

It's cold. Everyone has their head down and is getting on with it. The only people trying to meet my eyes are beggars. Some have coloured bibs and clipboards.

At least I know who I am now. Years ago, I remember an awkward conversation with one of the more reasonable promoters in which he was explaining why he wouldn't book me.

'I just don't know who you are' he repeated.

What he meant was, that although all the bits of my act worked, I wasn't saying or doing anything unique. I can see that now.

On the face of it you have a lot of choices. Whether to be blokey, girly, observational, quirky, manic, laconic, a storyteller, high status, low status, a gag machine, political, surreal, earthy or to spout streams of consciousness. You might combine one or several of these with an instrument, a puppet, props, impressions, magic or some kind of ethnic angle. But in a way you won't have a choice.

In the same way that a routine or a line evolves after a few outings in front of a crowd, your persona will find you too. It will also be part you, part monster. An alter ego that can seep into your personal life and both enliven and poison your relationships. Also, thinking about it, most acts can be summarised in three words – 'my blokey life', 'I'm weird, me', 'foreigners speak funny' etc.

A white van has just hooted at a couple of underdressed girls out on a lunch-hour. I wonder if that's ever worked – if a girl's ever thought to herself 'Oooh there's a man who knows how to use a car horn, *and* with his own drain cleaning business as well!'

In the street the only forms of communication are unwelcome ones. A flutist plays a tune to a backing track, hopping from note to note like a butterfly. Perhaps beggars should try backing tracks, of groans, general suffering or babies crying.

The camera is set up in a hotel room. Apparently I'm the fifth person they've seen this morning. Maggie the Producer greets me at the door; she seems to have recently left college after studying combined media and enthusiasm.

'Hello. You must be Jerome? Thanks so much for coming. Did you get the tape?'

'Yes thanks – one hundred greatest . . . children's animated stories.'

'Greatest Documentaries!'

'Documentaries were they? You mean that thing about the twin towers was true!? . . . . It's okay I'm only joking.'

'Thank goodness for that.'

So I'm to be a talking head on Channel 4's One Hundred Greatest Documentaries, but I've got a feeling that the one we're making won't be making the top thousand. They sent me a tape before the weekend with all sorts of short clips from factual TV programmes from over the last 30 years.

That beggar's asleep! His sign shouldn't say 'Hungry and Homeless', it should say 'Back in 10 minutes'!

The day didn't start well. The milk flew off my Crunchy Nut

Cornflakes sideways onto my lap. Then Marita flew into a rage for some reason. What does she want? She doesn't have to work; I'm bringing in the money.

The cameraman changes the film and the soundman mics. me up.
    None of this scares me anymore. Then an older woman opens a big metal box and begins to make me up like a corpse.

Now I have the self-belief to perform, the confidence to launch out and know that I will succeed, and even if I don't, that somehow I'll turn that failure into success. It's a mixture of science and sport – a contest to come up with a successful formula in any given situation. You can study styles and techniques but it's essentially an instinct. A muscle you develop.

She asks a question then I have to answer it incorporating the question into my reply. That's how it works – I've done this before. The trick is to come up with a sound bite that tells the audience what they've just seen and then to sum it up with some sort of clever comment. But it's difficult to do that without saying something you don't mean. I've already accused Kate Adie of starting the Gulf War single-handed and called John Pilger, John Pillock. This is cheap laughs at the expense of real heroes – well it is the lazy way I'm doing it.
    But, isn't the idea flawed in itself – to put in order of merit a catalogue of commentating on suffering? (And has anyone ever met a person who's voted on one of these things?)

Somewhere there's an itch I can't scratch. Something is gnawing at the edge of my leprous conscience. Are my nerves too numb to notice, and my brain too tired to care?
    The next homeless person I see I'll give him this ten-pound note. Where are they when you want them?

The producer seems to have a preconceived idea about what she wants me to say, and if I don't say it first time, she just asks me the same question again in a slightly different form. In the end I just say what I think they want, to get out of the room. Someone should make a documentary about it. All in all I'm not quite sure why I'm doing this. Oh yes, two hundred quid.

There's one! Perhaps I should just offer to buy him food, don't want to support his habit.
    'No, really, anything you want mate.'
    'Quail eggs!'
    Nice one.

A couple of months ago, Spaz asked me to help write on his TV show. Of course I leapt at it, the hunger is still there, if anything it's more desperate. The premise of *Losing It* is that Spaz charms his way undercover into an establishment organisation and then proceeds to test their patience, cause a scene and then sooner or later get fired. All in full view of hidden cameras, but in the name of exposing prejudice to mental illness of course. A few of us sent in some choice lines, but in fairness he came up with most of it on the spot. (Having snuck into the Queen's household as a footman, Spaz turns to her equerry and asks 'Is it just me, or does the Queen's face look like a coin?' That was one of mine.) It's a cult success and catapults its hero on his way to deserved stardom. It's no big deal for me – didn't even have to cancel a gig. But things are speeding up with this, the radio and talk of allsorts of other stuff.

Now I'm in Harrods just about to buy some quail's eggs. I can't wait to see that homeless guy's face. He'd better still be there. Well, he won't have gone home will he?

But Marita wants to know why everything has to be a joke. She says she can't go on living like this. She says she doesn't know who I am anymore.

Prison ₵ ₵ ₵ ₵ II

Bruce is snoring now. I'm glad he feels so comfortable in my company, that he's able to take me for granted. Well that can happen when you've known someone a while.

Perhaps I've let Marita down, and over the years morphed into someone else. Maybe I started out like Russell Crowe in *Gladiator*, but gradually turned into Gollum in the *Lord of the Rings*, obsessed with work and my 'precious' career.

One night in a bar after a show, in Singapore I think it was, I meet a deep-sea diver. (This comes out in conversation; he isn't wearing all his gear, obviously.) The stewardesses who were part of our group earlier have drifted away, and left us surrounded by glasses and gazing out on the harbour and the twinkly lights of the skyscrapers.

We have a surprising amount in common. Two mercenaries taking on tricky gigs all over the world – going where the money is. The perils of being freelance. (Just stopped myself asking him if he was keeping his head above water.) The main difference being, of course, that once again he has one of those jobs that puts his actual life in danger instead of just his pride and reputation. We laugh about this too, although on reflection it's probably funnier for me.

'You sound like a pretty experienced comedian' he ventures.

I snort because of the connotation of the phrase from the listings. But then taking it the way he means it, I agree.

But just then before heading off to the Gents, he says, soberingly 'And I'll bet your marriage has broken up as well!'

Smiling thinly, I mumble 'Not yet actually . . . not yet.'

End

April 2003: Car back from Cambridge

I'm driving on a motorway somewhere. Hardly remember how I got here. Various edits of the day are playing back and forth across the windscreen. Some on fast forward, some in slo-mo high definition.

The hearse glides up alongside the house. There it is. The coffin we chose, pine with gold handles. She's in there. Can't talk. Someone sniffs, it sets us all off.

The church is not far. Keith and Zoe walk hand in hand behind the limo. They look very alone. This is an alien ritual, but we all seem to know exactly what to do, to follow somberly.

Oh Suzy, are you in there? Are you looking down on us?

Just then Zoe turns round and pulls a face at me. For a second I freeze unsure of the etiquette. Then I pull a face back.

The service passes. There was no point in me even trying to say anything from up the front. My flowery yellow tie is the best I can do to stand up to the sudden brutality of death.

As I glance sideways Mum and Dad seem to have aged 10 years. Dad is shaking. The church is packed: mums from school, doctors from the clinic and lots of patients. She brought brightness to them all. Then a nurse and an old school friend go up and tell us exactly that. Zoe seems curiously unaffected. She is piling up prayer cushions to make a tower. Keith is just staring ahead. No one will tell her off today.

We all knew it was coming. She'd wasted away since the winter, since the doctors washed their hands of her. She sat in the armchair with a view of the garden, drowsy from painkillers, looked after by Keith and a Macmillan nurse who popped in from time to time. Mum and Dad stayed at a Bed and Breakfast nearby.

To save trouble I pretended to be working in Cambridge, but actually made the trip from London everyday to take Zoe to the swings. Perhaps I should have cancelled all my shows that week, but I kept putting it off not wanting to think that the next time I went to work, my sister would be dead.

Keith phoned me at home around seven on a sunny April morning. She hadn't woken up. We'd already said our goodbyes, but now this is the signal for the steam train of grief to get rolling. Later I go round to Mum and Dad's – and we hug and cry for a while.

In the days before the funeral, there's a lot of organising to do. But it's organising punctuated by tears, sniffles, the odd uncontrollable animal-like howl. Previously I'd thought I'd be able to channel my grief – tidy the house, get fit, or write a hilarious routine about grieving. But in the event it all seems pointless. And crying is surprisingly tiring.

The last time I saw her we didn't say anything profound. We had a cup of tea and scoffed at *Neighbours* on TV. She'd tried to speak to me a few days before though, as I helped her round the park. We sat on a bench and stared ahead. A blackbird swooped across the path sending out a warning that sounded like a rusty pair of scissors. Then Suzy said, as if she had prepared it, that she wanted to make sure that Zoe grew up understanding how to be really silly.

'Thanks very much' I said pretending not to understand. But she didn't have to spell it out. Keith is an excellent Dad. But he would never meet a passenger off a plane with a cardboard sign saying 'Fathead', or when stopped by clipboard carriers in the High Street, shout 'Boh!' in their faces (okay that's Stan's material).

Oh to be Italian, just for a week. To put my arms around her and tell her how proud I was, and that I loved her and that I was so sorry and angry; angry that this was one bully I couldn't duff up for her. Instead it came out in awful cricketing terms. I talked about a 'fantastic effort' and a 'brilliant innings'. Putting a stiff arm on her shoulder, I decided that if I didn't hold it together it would look like I knew the 'game was up'. So it's true: we English are too detached from our emotions to release them in the natural course of life, we need ritualised excuses like binge drinking, football hooliganism and stand-up comedy.

We sat in silence on a bench for a while and watched some old folks throw bread to the birds, as a squirrel bobbed and weaved across the grass as if avoiding silent gunfire. Anything, but facing what's about to happen.

That night as she watched Keith and Zoe reading each other *Winnie the Pooh*, I could tell she was saying goodbye.

At the graveside Dad sobs uncontrollably. It's his little girl after all. Keith is quite white, and his Mum and Dad have taken an arm each and are murmuring consolation. Then I give him a hug. Hugs in films always seem to be full-bodied and enthusiastic, but this is more awkward. But in that moment I know I haven't quite done him justice, that there was always part of me that was jealous of him for taking away my little sister.

Zoe is staring into the open grave. I come down to her size.

'It's only her body' I say.

She looks up. 'What about her head?'

'. . . and her head.'

Suzy would have liked that.

With a surge of emotion I pick both Zoe and my Arthur up in my arms. They giggle. Then I have to lift them up high, so they don't see my tears. Goodbye my darling.

We go back to their house and order a large Chinese take-away and open a couple of wine boxes. But all the time it's as if Suzy could pop her head round the corner at any moment. That's the other slightly smaller curse of death – that you find yourself speaking uncontrollably in clichés.

'It won't be the same without her', 'It's what she would've wanted' etc. Even at the graveside during the committal I had the urge to glance sideways and see if a detective was watching at a distance, a detective who had a hunch about how Suzy really died. (I was at home; Keith can back me up on that.)

It's a paralysing sick-sour feeling in the pit of my stomach that can burst out at any moment. Grief for myself, for Mum and Dad, Keith, Zoe and for Suzy – that she had to leave on her own, like a balloon escaping from a fairground. It's unnerving to see her hat on the coat-stand, and her writing on the fridge calendar. Is she really that far away? So, that heckler came back then, didn't know he was beaten, had to ruin the show for everyone.

Police

April 2003: Car back from Hendon

A lmost home, but I can't remember the journey there or back. Once again it's as if the windscreen is a giant TV that flips between growing up, the funeral, what Keith's doing now, and earlier this evening.

The following night I have a longstanding date in the diary. Mick is a friend and knows what's happened and offers to replace me, but it's a chance to escape. It's strange, I feel a bit vulnerable returning to work – like going back to school with a new haircut.

The Ambassador Club is one I know well and is usually full of stag and hen dos. Tables surround the stage and the walls are painted red and yellow. I've had some of my best and worst gigs standing on this tiny four-foot by four-foot plinth. But tonight it's a private function – lots of blokes with suits, not smart suits, well worn, shabby ones – and there are only a few women. Mick the manager shakes my hand, and offers his condolences.

'What have we got here then?' I enquire on autopilot.

'Didn't anyone tell you – it's wall to wall Newham Police Dept.'

Of course, lots of tall, world-weary men and no black people. (Two actually.) Usually I would be wary of so much authority, but I've just been at a gig where the Grim Reaper was in the house.

A car sounds its horn behind me. The traffic light is green. I move off.

Condolences! What are they? After national tragedies they open books of condolences. But who reads them afterwards? You'd have to have real trouble sleeping. That's one thing I've learnt though, it doesn't matter how stiff and awkward someone is about mentioning your grief, you appreciate them trying. Even if you don't know what to say back. The worst thing is being ignored, pretending that nothing has happened.

There's no real MC. An inspector in civvies gets up on stage to a barrage of catcalls. He doesn't really know what to say, and I've had better intros.

'Well we've got a turn for you now. His name's Jerome Stevens. If he's not funny blame Adrian – he booked him.'

Beginning with the three police jokes I have, I get off to a flier. A bald man laughs in the wrong place.

'Hello, who do you think you are, Kojak?'

It doesn't even make sense but they love it. They trust me now, and I can get on with the rest of my act. But seeing so many people laughing again is therapeutic.

'If I'm going too fast, stop me, you usually do.'

More laughs. This is what I do for a living. Yes, I'm alive, life goes on. (Another cliché.)

There's something about my manner this evening, that's both confident and dismissive, as if I don't care – which seems to make it all the funnier. There's even a loud roar when I tell one laughing table 'Shut up, will you!'

Should think about winding up soon. Then two women, at the bar, who are very drunk, start to chip in. The crowd rise to the contest.

'What's this,' I gamble 'the dog section?'

Now that wouldn't have worked on another night, but this is the right time and the right place. A couple of times I deliberately take my foot off the gas and enjoy the pause. Delightfully, they often laugh at the set ups, promising a big pay off on the punchlines. In passing I hint that all policemen are corrupt. But instead of taking offence someone shouts 'More Champagne!'

This is the best kind of interaction. They're good sports. Even I am laughing out loud now. Nights like this are why I joined up.

Nearly missed my turn. A police van speeds the other way, full of my new mates. What happened to panda cars? Apparently there are just a few left in the wild now.

As I close I pontificate 'So if we meet again, perhaps in a dark alley or on the hard shoulder of a motorway, just remember that any-thing you say or do may be taken down and later used against you.'

More barracking.

'Listen, if you don't like it, I'll write up a report, and then do absolutely nothing about it!'

Applause and cheers: the best gig I've done for a while, for a number of reasons, and on reflection there are not many jobs in which you can insult 120 police for half an hour, they clap and cheer and then you get paid for it.

Just before I went on I had a call. Jim Bernstein's car has broken down and he can't get to a gig in Hendon. Can I cover for him? He has no idea what's happened to me recently, but that's not his fault, he'd happily do the same for me, besides, I'm on a roll. I like doubling up. You don't get a chance to think too much, and once you're out of the house you may as well work as hard as you can.

It turns out to be a show for a Jewish youth group. This could be tricky; they seem quite well off and judging by the ringlets and skullcaps some of them are quite orthodox. Let's hope they'll take to a gentile. Like in an old episode of *Star Trek*, I'll have to go in with my deflector shields down to look like I'm vulnerable, and then when they drop their guard I can get to work.

The crowd is lively. The MC speaks some Yiddish and they all laugh. Now it's me.

'Listen I'm not Jewish, but there's not much I can do about that – okay there is, but I'd really rather not . . .'

It works and I'm on my away again – they like me too. I can lose myself in the moment . . .

That's it! That's what it's all about – lifting people's spirits. Going into a dark room with the promise of delivering a gift. And if you manage to do so, it can be a healing meal of fun.

But about halfway through the Jewish gig, I come to another gag I've used for a while, about holidays for children with short attention spans, and making the mistake of advertising them as concentration camps.

On the night I don't do it, and do you know, I don't think I'll do it again.

Hungry, I stop for some chips on the way home. Some chips and a can of Sprite. The tin is lukewarm and there's a thin layer of dust on the surface. It's stood for months on a shelf in the shop. It lasted longer than she did.

Feeling heavy again. But I'm almost home now. She's still gone. And I forget to eat the chips.

School

June 2003: Stretch limo
back from Kingston

Okay, it's more of a bendy bus. But this is a familiar route, I used to do this journey to and from school everyday. I've just been back to talk to the Sixth Form about working in comedy.

The old place hasn't changed that much. Hang on, in my day I seem to remember it was all about getting grades. So now I'm heralded as an achiever because I muck about for a living? Has society changed that much? Well, I knew I was onto something. Yes, but I can't help feeling there should be some sort of official apology, and perhaps a plaque in the hall saying 'For all those who laid down their education to get cheap laughs from their friends'. Yeah and where are all the swots now eh? Probably helping provide fresh water for African villages and leading the field in pioneering heart surgery– losers!

The brakes hiss as we reach a stop, like someone opening a giant can of fizzy drink. The doors part and the bubbly young froth out onto the pavement, while the more experienced gather up their bags and pushchairs and calmly drip off the side into the High Street.

Just then – a glimpse of a turquoise skirt! My heart jumps!? Of course – St Hilda's, the girls' school! They still catch this bus. Those unattainable beauties whose eyes you would meet for a second and then build a whole fantasy around. For a second I imagine myself trying to do the same now. But hang on, these could be the daughters of the girls I knew. There's something wrong with that.

There are still a couple of teachers who I remember, but I'm not sure they remember me. To be fair I was pretty anonymous, in fact when I started doing drama in my last two years, more than one teacher thought I was a new pupil.

But now the staff seem more human, and it's the hordes of dishevelled teenagers that are alien. It's a relief to be shown into the quiet of the Headmaster's study to see Mr Keesing. I'm offered a coffee. Last time I was in here, it was for a bad report. The Head was different then and Wheezing Keesing was just head of Geography.

'Stevens isn't it?'

'Yes sir' I reply instinctively.

'You've done very well for yourself.'

'Thank you sir, so have you.'

He's a little greyer and dustier now, like what his older brother would look like if he'd just finished demolishing a wall. He shuffles some papers. He doesn't seem to know why I'm here does he? Someone's put him up to this.

'Remind me of the particular field of your success?'

'Oh, I'm just Britain's top Ofsted inspector.'

'Ah . . . yes it's comedy isn't it?'

It seems the school like to keep in contact with anyone who achieves in their field, or is that anyone who might provide money for a scholarship or the best part of a mini-bus – in which case they seem to have overestimated how much I'm making. Just because they heard me on the radio doesn't mean I've got a swimming pool. (It just means I can afford to go to one occasionally.) I like the idea of setting up an award though, for the best impersonation of a teacher, perhaps – that's how I started after all. And with a prize in keeping with setting off on a career in the arts – a *Big Issue* and a can of Special Brew.

Mucking about can be dangerous though. In the old days it was essays, detentions and failed exams. These days . . . well yesterday I went to see Spaz.

The door to his Docklands penthouse apartment was unlocked. I pushed it ajar against a pile of unopened post. He's bought the flat recently – outright with the money he got for some dog food ads. But lately he's disappeared after a series of bad gigs and some erratic behaviour.

He's also been hopelessly over-committing himself, saying he'll be in two places at once. He always did try and please everyone – talk to the crowd on the way out. Oh yes, and he attacked a man in Leeds! (For heckling – he didn't just get the train up there and punch someone!) We've all nearly done it, but now promoters don't know whether they can trust him.

'Spaz!' I shout, fearing the worst, and hoping to disturb the rats from his rotting corpse. In the living room the curtains are drawn and the whole place flickers to the images of a large TV screen. There's packaging everywhere. Flat-pack wardrobes still in their boxes, half eaten curries and enough empties to start a bottle-bank.

There he is, sitting in a chair in the middle of the room with food stains on his T-shirt.

'Hello mate!' he says as if he's been expecting me.

'Spaz! You're a mess, what's going on? You're not even answering your phone.'

'That's the thing about phones, exactly how small are they going to get?' he rambles, as if addressing a crowd.

He's high, low, drunk, mental or something. Or he's been addicted so long he's forgotten how to be sober, like a bike whose brakes have completely worn away. What am I going to do? It's like *Apocalypse Now* where Marlon Brando goes AWOL in the jungle. Except that was in Cambodia amongst the Killing Fields. Spaz has just spent too long in places like Nottingham, Glasgow and Maidstone trying to win the hearts and minds of locals who don't appear to have either. It probably doesn't help being paid thousands of pounds for pretending to be a dog either.

'Spaz, you need help mate.'

'Fifteen thousand quid.'

'What?'

'That's what I got for presenting some awards last night.'

'No, you didn't, you didn't turn up.'

'Didn't I? Jerome! How are the kids?'

'Fine.'

Then I remember that I'm annoyed with him, what was it, oh yes – last time he saw 'the kids', he described Arthur as being very 'tame' like he was some kind of small mammal. Although, perhaps if he had the stability of being in charge of a zoo like mine, he might not have got in this mess in the first place.

He continues to shoot off random sentences like a CD player on 'shuffle'. Then I phone his Mum and she arranges to come over and take him back to Guildford that afternoon. Guildford – that'll please him no end – it's what he started out talking about in his act years ago.

'If you re-arrange the letters of Guildford, you're probably so bored, you actually live in Guildford.' Well it was funny the way he said it.

Now Spaz is asleep in the chair. Shame, his TV show was good. *Losing It* won a couple of awards but it didn't get a second series due to its star's unreliability. We did make an MP resign though. Spaz went undercover as a representative of the Romany people in Britain and got a right wing Member of Parliament, seeking to be politically correct, to make an impassioned plea on camera to change the name of the biscuit Gypsy Creams to *Traveller Creams*. Apparently it was the last straw in a chequered career. But just for a second it felt like we'd affected the real world.

But recently Spaz has lost his instinctive charm, and he's gone from butterfly back to some awful chrysalis.

For a while he had an entourage that followed him round, but then there were tales of drugs, and kiss and tells in the papers and now they've all fled like ships from a sinking love rat. His relationships seem to have become shorter and shorter until now there's no one left. He's like Sellotape that's been relocated once too often and has finally lost all its stickiness. Most comics have a heyday. Two if they're lucky. Spaz will be back, I hope.

It's not that long since we passed through an airport together. He charmed his way through security – the toughest of crowds. Making hardened guards and weary passengers laugh out loud. Then he tied a label to his arm and sat on the luggage carousel as it went round and round, singing 'Nessun dorma' to the waiting crowd. By the end I was giddy with joy. That's what I want to remember about him. Not that he's dead. Yet.

Keith phoned earlier, said he was having a bad day, bursting into tears when he'd found some of Suzy's red hairs blocking up the vacuum cleaner. He did tell me a bit like he was reporting that the bakery section had run out of pitta breads – but I didn't care at all. I was glad. We're both a bit softer now.

Still, the birds are singing, I make a living telling jokes and my old school thinks I'm a success – it's a sunny day.

Just then some kids get on the bus. They're noisy, untidy and are speaking some sort of strange patois that's a mixture of cockney and predictive text. Staring resolutely out of the window I tut to myself and hope not to get stabbed. And yes, they're from my old school.

It all seemed so different then – the sky was blue, Curly Wurlys were eight pence and being a rebel was just turning up the collar on your blazer. Now they have sweatshirts instead of blazers – easier to wash the blood out of, I suppose. Yes, since then the double-decker bus of our dreams has ploughed under the low bridge of reality.

Prison ⦀⦀ ⦀⦀ ⦀⦀ III

I must have been here for nearly a day now surely. Let's see . . .

The door! Suddenly I'm wrestled to my feet by two guards. Bruce stays squatting in the corner. He looks away as I leave. Was that pity or contempt that crossed his face? Perhaps he knows what's going to happen to me. No one's telling me anything.

On to the pick-up truck and surrounded by soldiers. One man with a gun could probably keep me in check but as always no one can accuse the Chinese of under-manning. Twelve, no thirteen, all with rifles. A firing squad!? Where are we going? It's still daylight. Stay calm. I turned down my last meal. What would I order anyway? Bulletproof vest pie.

It's a long drive to wherever we're going, whether it's to my freedom, or a place of execution. Perhaps they're going to exchange me with a Chinese spy captured in the West. Should I try and make a run for it? But where to? I don't exactly blend in. Peasants on bicycles, weighed down with chickens and furniture, stop and stare.

Maybe I should wave, cause a fuss, shout obscenities – now, for some reason, I'm going through my act in my head. Yes, it's like I'm on my way to a gig. Literally a gig for a firing squad. Please God may the place burn down before I get there.

What's that old joke about the Englishman, Scotsman and Irishman all facing a firing squad. The Irishman shouts 'fire fire'. That's the punch line. The others shout 'earthquake' and things. I could close with that. If I get that far. No one will know it's not my gag. That's if I don't go into my 'slanty little eyes' routine before then. Shouldn't I be making peace with my maker rather than thinking what gags to do?

Now we're coming into the main town. They wouldn't kill me here surely. Unless they hold executions in a public square, or at a football stadium at half time. We round the corner. There's the gig! I recognise the bar. Oh, is this my public humiliation before they take me off never to be seen again? I could make a run for it, but my heart is beating so fast I'd probably overbalance. When it comes to it, I freeze terrified and helpless. Dry mouth, legs of lead.

'Where are you taking me? I'm a British citizen' I hear someone say. It's me.

'I've got a family.'

The last part of the word 'family' disappears under a croak. This is it, one way or the other. I close my eyes. So despite years of fantasising about what I'd do in a life or death situation, it turns out I just want my Mummy like everyone else. I thought in that final moment I would be at peace with the world, like a contestant who runs out of luck on a game show . . .

'Well, I've had a lovely time Chris . . .'

Instead I'm terrified and it's as cold and as grim as I could have imagined. Not funny at all. I think of my family.

The pick-up stops, I'm ordered out. All I can hear is my heart. And breathing.

The pick up drives off. Now I'm alone in the road.

I cough and take a deep breath or two. Didn't think they'd shoot me. Of course they wouldn't. Then after finally catching my breath I try and walk as nonchalantly as I can into the nearest Starbucks.

Nothing To Declare

July 2004: White water raft,
Eastern Canada, downstream

N ot so much a river, more like a horizontal waterfall (Niagara isn't far away, I suppose). But this is an oasis compared to the whirlpool of the Montreal Comedy Festival. A few of us have travelled 30 miles upstate on our day off for a breath of fresh air.

It's an honour to be asked to represent your country, apparently, and a few months ago I would have jumped at the opportunity. But my 'one-man-show' in a Chinese prison has only just finished its controversial run, and it's Marita who persuades me to take the risk of offending some other foreigners. Mum and Dad bravely volunteer to come up from Kent to house sit – entering the forest of coloured plastic and eternal crying to keep an eye on the naughty elves for a week.

Visiting North America is like being on television. The buildings, the traffic and the food make you feel as if you're playing a minor role in some detective series. Inevitably, however, the people are slightly uglier than you'd been led to believe. Canada is like America on a public holiday. Lower key, but the same cars – the ones with whole bits of wood stuck to the sides. Montreal is a bit more stylish and aloof like the French who settled here.

All the comics and agents are housed in one hotel – the Belmont. They take over the place for two weeks and all the prices are raised accordingly. Comics are here from all over the world for all sorts of highly organised shows.

We receive our safety instructions from Kai, a large mountain woodsman. He doesn't look like he would suffer comedians gladly. 'Six-four, native American, a hundred and eighty pounds, armed and dangerous' the police report would say, if and when he can take no more of our banter and goes crazy with a mountain knife. But it turns out he has a routine of his own – the safety talk is a five minute open spot.

'I am the Last of the Mohicans, all my tribe ignored the safety instructions . . . . Emergency exits are . . . all over the place . . . you have to hang on tight!'

We all smile obligingly. Now is not the time to tell him we're comedians too. We aren't the stars here, we're punters – punters who could die. It turns out this is actually quite dangerous. We sign waivers to cover the company should we not make it, and I think about adding a clause asking Mum and Dad to bring up the kids.

Dave Schnauzer is an American comic who has been going eight years. He's delighted to be here, having showcased for Montreal three times and now he's finally made it. He has a slick seven minutes about midgets and travelling on aeroplanes ('. . . at least you don't feel so bad about putting your seat back when there's a little guy behind you' etc). He's looking for a TV development deal, and he definitely wasn't planning on looking death in the eye this morning. His perfect smile has dimmed for a bit.

The shows have been straightforward enough – enthusiastic crowds. But the comedy on offer is not cutting edge and there are depressingly few taking any sort of risk. Last night I saw a woman from the festival sitting backstage with a small metal clicker-like thing in her hand, which she clicked every time there was a roar from in front of the curtains. She was counting the laughs without even watching the show! Again, laughter is just a commodity here, like fuel or beer.

There's also a huge difference in the tone of the British acts compared to the Americans. The Yanks tend to play winners, manicured and shiny – 'Don't you just hate it when . . .' comedy. Whereas the Brits' default setting is low status, putting themselves down – 'I'm crap because . . .' stuff. You can almost hear the Americans in the audience thinking 'Should we be laughing at this guy? He's a loser'.

We're all in a raft that's out of control. Involuntary screams. These paddles are useless. We hit rocks and currents, we spin and shriek and surge and crash. It's another, possibly more realistic analogy, of our careers. At least I have Marita with me.

Just to seal the comparison, as we disembark Dave falls in, so I jump in after him. Not in any heroic way really, but just to give him a hand out, but he's already panicking. As he tries to get to the shore he pushes down on my head and I disappear for a second under the foam. It's not a problem; I've got a crash helmet and a lifejacket on, besides I can swim. Even so, Marita screams 'Watch what you're doing!'

Bobbing up in the froth I wink at her, amused and slightly touched by her concern. She rolls her eyes, and looks away. She still cares then.

'Sorry man I just lost it out there' Dave begins, and then he jaws on about himself again.

A lot of water has passed by but here we stand, one of us aloof, and the other up to his neck in it. She wades in and pulls me out and kisses me on the lips. We still have each other.

Yesterday Michael, one of the Montreal organisers, came up to me in the bar.

'I have some exciting news.'

'Really?'

'The people from Fox would like to meet you for breakfast.'

'*Breakfast!?*' I reply like Uncle Eddie.

'Yes, they're very busy people.'

'Er . . .'

In the past perhaps my heart would have leapt at this information, but I don't seem to care so much now.

'We've booked white water rafting tomorrow, and we've got to leave early.'

'Sorry Jerome, I don't think you heard me; the *Fox people* want to have breakfast with you! You can go white water rafting anytime!'

There's something in his veneration of the 'Fox people' that makes me dig in. Not only does it make me think of a collection of strange furry executives with pointy features, but it also rankles that he suddenly expects me to jump up and down at the pitter-patter of their tiny paws.

'No we *can't* go white water rafting anytime. This is our only day off. On the other days we can't get back in time to do the show!'

Michael leaves shaking his head and saying he'll see what he can do. But for the first time on this trip I feel as if I've said something funny.

That night the 'me me me circus' continues in the bar downstairs, like that place in the garden near the compost, where all the flies seem to gather. Upstairs Marita and I lie naked in bed eating tortilla chips, deciding to take the kids to the States and Disneyland, but not to tell them until we get to the airport. We can't help giggling when we think of their little faces.

Then Marita laughs again when she recalls the breakfast we all had together before we left. Reg had shouted 'rubbish' to a joke I'd tried, and then he began to quote in a silly singsong voice: 'You never failed to shout "rubbish" when I was rubbish and often we laughed together like friends.' (He must have found that note I wrote in prison.) I chased him out of the house and down the street in my dressing gown – but I was laughing like I haven't laughed for a very long time.

Sweeping the crumbs of tortilla out of the sheets I have another realisation.

'I don't know what it is' I begin. 'Recently a huge weight has been lifted off my shoulders.'

'It was Dave Schnauzer' scoffs Marita, and then she sighs.

We carry on, laughing and thinking out-loud together. This is how it should be. Saying things, then saying other things by not saying stuff – like jazz. We've been through some things, her and me. Just then I notice my wife's hands. They're girl's hands. I pick one up and begin to kiss it again . . . .

The next night I find an ally in Adam Lennister, an up and coming Scottish act. All the Americans are making sure they are preceded by a host of credits in order to fanfare their arrival. We make up our own, and the MC dutifully repeats them.

'This guy's from London, he played Edie McCredie the heroin addict in *Balamory*, and has just finished filming his own series on the TV in the window of Dixons at the Arndale Centre!'

It's gibberish, but we, and a few Brits in the crowd, enjoy it. It's like winning some sort of moral victory.

When we get back I'm going out for a drink with Ralph. Well, I left a message on his answer-phone the other day and eventually he texted back saying 'R U still a tosser?'!

It's the first time in a long while that I don't know what to reply.

Changed Priorities Ahead

November 2004: Car from home to Guffaw Bar One

The traffic flows freely until Kings Cross. But this time I'm happy to sit in the road works, taking in the coloured lights and the noise. Everyone's sitting tight in their little metal cubicles – pairs of chairs in a tin, stopping and starting in the wet – cells that are free to go where they like.

Now we're moving again. Turning off, I park at the end of a side road. Sitting in the car I take in the glow from the club a hundred yards away. Pulled towards it, I check myself briefly, renewing my vow to spend more time at home, to occasionally eat whole packets of biscuits, and sometimes just to sit and stare at the sky. Tomorrow I've turned down a gig in order to play badminton with Ralph. Getting out, I can just hear the distant waves of laughter crashing again and again over the stage. Swinging the car door shut, I put my bag under my arm and set off once more towards the surf.

Inside, the first act, Steve 'Animal' Hatter, is haranguing a man with silver hair.

'You're old and going to die soon' he shouts.

The crowd cackle in disbelief. But there's method to this

invective, each shocking idea surprising like a burst pipe in a submarine.

A few minutes later the untamable firebrand is off stage and filling in his VAT form. But just then the old boy comes up and tries to land a punch, catching Steve on the shoulder, but security have the assailant out in the street in a matter of seconds.

'I only wanted to hit him' he shouts. Fair enough.

Looking round there's a noisy group of lads with jugs of beer on their table. The younger ones can still tuck their shirts into their trousers, the others wear them loose, like sheets covering part of them that's died. But they're having fun. Apparently it's a works do, for a publication for firefighters. Didn't know such things existed. There must be something there . . .

The prison seems a long time ago now, although it's only been a few months. Of course there was no diplomatic incident, I was only there for an embarrassing 19 hours – not even a whole day, a real storm in a teacup. But I wouldn't like to go through it again, not for all the teacups in China.

When Gerry eventually arrived to pick me up from Starbucks he was livid and keen to take it further, but I just wanted to go home. We flew back to Shanghai that afternoon. Then I had a shower, a sleep, and even did the show the night after.

Sometimes I wonder what happened to Bruce Leak. Did he get put on a lorry too, but was never seen again? Or is he still in the same cell, singing 'Aw Wi Suvi'? That bucket must be pretty full by now.

Apparently my detention was all about turf wars. The bar hadn't paid its bribe to the requisite local official and the good Chairman was just demonstrating a bit of muscle on behalf of his warlord. The joke was on me. But I'm not sure who had the last laugh – according to Gerry, the Chairman disappeared soon after, and there was talk of corruption charges.

I played the whole thing down to my family, although obviously for fellow comics I've turned it into a cartoon – a slick three-minute routine with about six different laughs. But to be honest, if I took tea with Nelson Mandela I probably wouldn't mention it.

It's the interval before I go on. Someone's passed out near the bar, there's another fight happening outside, and a couple emerge unashamed from a cubicle in the Gents.

A few days ago I went to see Arthur in his nursery Christmas play. He was an angel who tells the shepherds the good news. But when it gets to his eagerly awaited line there's a moment of hesitation. It's the first time my stomach has turned over since China. Someone gives him a dig and then he remembers.

On reflection the whole prison experience was an elbow in the ribs for me too. A short sharp enema to the brain, which restored some lost perspective. At least Arthur didn't shout 'Come on you towel heads', or some other kind of racial slur, like his Dad might have done. Still not sure where that came from, just a desperate hitting out I think. Who knows what lurks within.

As I drove here tonight I forgot to look at the Hammersmith Apollo – apparently Mickey Spinola has extended his run there. Not so long ago that would have upset me, but tonight the bitterness just isn't there. Okay, maybe a bit.

But I'm tired of all that, and maybe my priorities have changed. After all it's just jokes. Perhaps no one writes them at all. Maybe there are millions just out there, hidden by angels in our collective subconscious, and once found they can be used like ancient herbal remedies, one for every incongruity known to man. Comedians are just the quacks who bother to dig them up in kit-form, construct them as best they can, and then use them again and again and again.

I'll be on as soon as they've served everyone at the bar. Now The MC's back on stage, settling them down.

Oh, and in the end I had that meeting in Canada with the 'Fox people'. They weren't the half men, half feral dogs I was expecting, but seemed quite genuine in their appreciation of the whole seven minutes they'd seen me do. We agreed to stay in touch and perhaps one day we'll 'do lunch' (an unsuspecting chicken perhaps).

But even if it all comes together for me or Spaz or one of the others, we might well end up looking back on our time on the circuit as the best years, the years where night after night we walked unknown, into cold and dismal rooms and then more often than not, deliberately set the place alight.

The disconcerting thing about this venue is that on stage sometimes you can catch a glimpse of yourself, in a mirror at the back of the room. Usually I try and ignore this because, I suppose, it's a reminder that you're just a man saying words. But if that happens tonight, it won't matter at all, because recently I've realised that's exactly the beauty of it – that I'm just a man saying words.

Now is a good time to be a comic, and London is the place to be. They say it's like the creative explosion of music in the 1960s. A gold rush, where prospectors from all over the world have set up camp. Every night of the week, wit sparkles all over the capital. There's also plenty of idiot's silver about too, but that's what makes it all so fascinating.

Also this evening, as I swept down the A40, I went past a poster for a Hollywood blockbuster. One face looks familiar. It's that American open spot from a few months ago. I guess he got that audition in LA. (That was quick!) Good for him. And to think, he was in my car once!

How will history judge us? Well that depends if it's written by the hecklers, or those who appreciate what it's like to have a go. In time the young will invent their own form of comedy that my generation won't understand. Working comics who are any good, and still have the appetite, will adapt and survive as best they can. Others will retire hurt and disaffected. Perhaps then the hectoring voices of what was once the circuit will seem strangely quaint and insular. Political correctness will be just another archaic code of behaviour like medieval chivalry or kabuki, taught as history or put on as a display for tourists.

'Watch how the heckler shouts "boo" repeatedly, as he perceives the comedian to have made a racist remark which, believe it or not, was frowned on in those days!'

As I look round the room everybody is smiling and seems to be having a good time. It may be contrived, but this isn't such a bad business to be in. Of course comedians take risks, but no one really dies. Perhaps it's a soft life, inconsequential. It's not providing fresh water for villages in the desert, or inventing a special valve that saves people from heart attacks – although in its own way, I like to think, it's both these things.

Sure, applause is like a fizzy drink that, if you take in too much, can have a strange effect on your behaviour. But if you're determined, and you can learn to take the affirmation and rejection with equal detachment, stand-up can be a fabulous curse to live with.

The MC is winding up again; the audience is being primed to give me a chance. Here we go, this is here and now, and it's just between me and them. A publication for firefighters, it would be handy to have something . . . . *Heat* magazine, that'll do – yes I can do something with that. The intro music is getting louder . . . here we go.

Success or not, I'm not sure it gets much better than this. Who knows where we're all going, (that reminds me I've got a corporate in Finland next week) but I'm enjoying the ride and the bed is broken from our family jumping up and down on it. Fantastic job, fantastic life: you've been a great audience, safe journey, thank you and goodnight!